PRESSURE POLITICS

PRESSURE POLITICS

MARTIN J SMITH

baseline
BOOKS

First published 1995 by
Baseline Book Company
PO Box 34
Chorlton
Manchester M21 1LL

British Library Cataloguing in Publication Data

ISBN 1 897626 07 X

Cover design   Ian Price
Cover illustration   Min Cooper
Typesetting   Kathryn Holliday
Printed and bound by Nuffield Press, Oxford

ACKNOWLEDGEMENTS

I would like to thank Fiona Devine who again provided help beyond the call of duty
and Mike Kenny for supplying some of the information on new social movements. **MJS**

CONTENTS

ABBREVIATIONS

AUEW	Allied Union of Electrical Workers
BEIC	British Eggs Industry Council
BMA	British Medical Association
BSE	Bovine spongiform encephalopathy
CAP	Common Agricultural Policy
CBI	Confederation of British Industry
CND	Campaign for Nuclear Disarmament
COPA	Committee of Professional Agricultural Organisations
DHA	District Health Authority
DHSS	Department of Health and Social Security
DoE	Department of the Environment
DoH	Department of Health
EC	European Community
ECJ	European Court of Justice
EP	European Parliament
ESC	Economic and Social Committee
EU	European Union
FDF	Food and Drink Federation
FDIC	Food and Drink Industries Council
FMF	Food Manufacturers' Federation
FoE	Friends of the Earth
IoD	Institute of Directors
LEA	Local Education Authority
MAFF	Ministry of Agriculture, Fisheries and Food
MSC	Manpower Services Commission
NCC	National Consumers Council
NEDC	National Economic Development Council
NFU	National Farmers' Union
NHS	National Health Service
NSM	New social movement
NUM	National Union of Mineworkers
OECD	Organisation for Economic Cooperation and Development
QMV	Qualified majority voting
RPM	Retail Price Maintenance
RSPB	Royal Society for the Protection of Birds
SEA	Single European Act
TUC	Trades Union Congress

INTRODUCTION

The Criminal Justice Bill, the roads programme, VAT on fuel, water quality and disabled rights are all policy areas in which the government has faced substantial pressure from a range of interest groups in recent years. The 1990s appears to be the decade of the pressure group. Pressure groups are growing in both membership and numbers. Nearly all policy areas involve pressure groups of one kind or another, and whenever the government develops policy in a new area it contacts pressure groups for advice, views and information. This book analyses the changing nature of pressure politics.

PRESSURE GROUP GROWTH

Pressure groups have had considerable success in recent years. Abolition of the poll tax, reduction of lead in petrol, cessation by ferry companies of live-animal transportation, strengthening of controls on water pollution and reduction of the age of consent for homosexuals have all been the product, to some extent, of pressure group politics.

It is now argued that we are entering an era of anti-politics in which pressure groups are the dominant mode of political representation and expression.[1] People are abandoning traditional modes of representation through political parties and joining pressure groups instead. They are increasingly disillusioned with politicians and parties, with broken promises, hypocrisy, lack of principle and absence of any clear distinction between the major parties' policies. They are, therefore, turning from political parties to groups that represent their interests more directly. Labour Party membership fell from more than a million in the 1950s to just over 200,000 in 1992. Conservative party membership fell from a reported 2.8 million in 1960 to 750,000 in 1989.

Whilst party membership has declined, that of pressure groups has increased dramatically. Membership of environmental groups more than doubled to more than four million in the 1980s. The National Trust now has more members than the three major parties put together. Membership of the Royal Society for the Protection of Birds (RSPB) increased from about 20,000 in 1965 to 860,000 in 1992.

Friends of the Earth (FoE) has increased its membership from some 1000 people in the 1960s to around 200,000 today.[2]

Pressure group success seems to be bringing individuals who would not otherwise be active into the political arena. Campaigns to prevent new roads being built through Twyford Down in Hampshire and across Oxleas Wood in east London have seen new alliances develop between 'alternative' New Age groups, such as the Donga Tribe, and middle-class homeowners. In some cases, 'respectable' and established individuals have been prepared to resort to direct action in an attempt to stop roads being built.

The 1980s and 1990s have witnessed the growth of a range of radical and alternative pressure groups, particularly in response to Labour's failure to challenge the Conservative monopoly on power. Groups such as anti-apartheid campaigners, the Campaign for Nuclear Disarmament (CND) and Greenpeace have been prepared to use demonstrations and direct action to challenge the government and influence the political agenda. To some degree they have been successful. Anti-apartheid groups encouraged a consumer boycott of South African goods and increased the pressure on government to continue sanctions. CND made nuclear weapons a political issue. Greenpeace played a role in forcing government to develop a more effective environmental policy.

Increasingly pressure groups are covering the political domain. They are particularly active in the policy spheres of animal rights, rights of the disabled, human rights, gay rights, and all forms of environmental and anti-nuclear protest. Many of the groups that have sprung up in these areas are concerned with what might be called citizenship issues, rather than with economic concerns. Often their goal is recognition of rights to citizenship and of a legitimate place in society.

There has also been a growth of groups involved in so-called 'lifestyle' politics. These are groups concerned with issues of identity, rights and personal freedom. Often they attempt to show that certain individuals have particular identities and lifestyles, and that they have the right to pursue these ways of life. Thus, groups such as Stonewall have campaigned for gays, groups like People First and the advocacy movement have begun campaigns to establish rights for the disabled and to show that the disabled can organise themselves and are not dependent on others.

Frequently these groups do not use traditional patterns of pressure group politics. They do not lobby government but seek to develop self-help networks.[3] The self-advocacy movement is concerned with developing forums within which the disabled can learn what their rights are and find out how to make their own cases and representations to official bodies. It has been inspired by the 'People First' philosophy which is not interested in obtaining special treatment but with ensuring that the disabled have the same rights as everyone else. The goal is normalisation and getting service providers to listen to those with learning difficulties, rather than professionals, about what they want and desire. The group aims to be user-led and independent of government and local authority bodies. It therefore seeks to develop self-help networks and to encourage those with learning difficulties to press for their own needs to be met rather than relying on social workers and state provision.[4] The advocacy movement demonstrates how new types of groups have developed and the way in which they have been concerned not only with lobbying government but with establishing independent networks of self-help.

CHANGING PRESSURE GROUPS

The growth in the range and size of pressure groups is a relatively new phenomenon. Pressure groups have been important to government throughout the post-war period but what has changed is the range and type of pressure groups which exists. Traditionally, politics has been dominated by economic groups, such as the trade unions, business, and professional groups, such as the British Medical Association (BMA). These groups had either direct economic power or information that government needed and so were given direct access to the policy process.

Social and political change, increased education, the availability of more information, economic problems and disillusionment with traditional politics, seem to have resulted in more people joining diverse groups that are concerned not only with occupational and economic interests but with questions of rights and specific causes.

These groups have had some undoubted successes. Yet it is important not to exaggerate the changes that have occurred. To a large degree, many of the changes that government makes are likely to be marginal and symbolic rather than fundamental changes in policy. Although replacement of the poll tax was largely the result of pressure group activity – which had a marked effect on the perceptions of Conservative MPs – other apparent pressure group success may, in fact, have other causes. The removal of cruise missiles from Greenham Common had more to do with the end of the Cold War than with pressure group activity. There is a tendency for both politicians and probably pressure groups to exaggerate the impact that groups have.

It must also be remembered that Margaret Thatcher was very suspicious of pressure groups. She believed that they were concerned only with protecting their own narrow interests, demanding more public expenditure and distorting the functioning of the market. Therefore, despite increased pressure group activity in certain years, much of the observable activity might be the result of frustration at a lack of access rather than a demonstration of increasing influence.

Indeed, certain groups have done particularly badly in recent years. Most evidently, the trade unions, which were central to economic policy making in the 1960s and 1970s, have been almost completely excluded from the policy process since 1979. They have also had their power actively reduced by legislation. Professional groups, such as doctors and teachers, have also had much less influence over the development of policy than they had in the 1970s. Rather than looking to professional groups, government has turned to managers, think tanks and consumers of public services. The poverty lobby and welfare groups also lost influence in the 1980s.

ASSESSING PRESSURE GROUP ACTIVITY

It has to be remembered that pressure group visibility is not the same as pressure group success. Some groups may be noisy and well-supported, but they are not necessarily influential. Getting media attention is not the same as influencing policy. Indeed, often it is not the well-known and popular pressure groups which have the ear of policy makers. Instead, government is more likely to listen to well-informed, respectable groups that are prepared to make their case by quiet contact with civil servants over a long period. It is groups that do not try to embarrass government over the long term that are likely to have the necessary access to influence policy. Government wants information, not propaganda.

It is also important to remember that even very large groups do not represent the majority of people. Those who are members of pressure groups tend to be highly educated and middle class. In this sense pressure groups are not at all representative of the British people as a whole. Although green groups have been very good at raising the profile of environmental issues and the impact of western lifestyles on global resources, the indication is that most people still want to buy material goods that are not necessarily ecologically efficient. Similarly, whilst there may be very vocal opposition to the government's road programme, the majority of car users may, in fact, be in favour of extra motorway lanes and new by-passes.

For these reasons it can be argued that pressure groups are not necessarily an unqualified democratic good. They can distort the political agenda by raising an issue which is of concern to a vocal minority but not the 'silent' majority. They distort the democratic process by persuading policy makers to adopt policies which are not supported by the majority of people. In a world in which pressure groups are central to the policy process, it is the well-organised, well-resourced and strategically-important interests which tend to influence government, not those which have the most justifiable claims on government attention and time. Pressure groups do not necessarily enhance the democratic process.

To understand pressure groups it is necessary to place them in context. The aim of this book is to highlight how the influence of pressure groups often depends on factors beyond their control. The impact they have on the policy process depends on social factors, the ideology of key actors and the goals of politicians and civil servants. Even well-resourced groups may fail to secure influence if they do not establish the right relationship with government.

NOTES

1 G Mulgan, *Politics in an Antipolitical Age* (Polity, Cambridge, 1994).
2 These figures come from P Seyd and P Whiteley, *Labour's Grass Roots* (Oxford University Press, Oxford, 1992); P Webb, 'The United Kingdom' in R S Katz and P Mair, *Party Organisations* (Sage, London, 1992); S Young, *The Politics of the Environment* (Baseline Books, Manchester, 1993); 'A Nation of Groupies', *Economist*, 13 August 1994.
3 See A Lent and M Sowemimo, 'Thatcherism and the Changing Face of Opposition Politics' in S Ludlam and M J Smith, *Contemporary British Conservatism* (Macmillan, Basingstoke, 1995).
4 Thanks to Rohhss Chapman for this information.

1 THE NATURE AND ROLE OF PRESSURE GROUPS

In constitutional textbooks, Britain is characterised as a parliamentary democracy. Parliament is sovereign. It cannot be bound by its predecessors, and there is no higher authority. However, with the growth of party discipline in the late-nineteenth century, the executive became the dominant institution within parliament. The dominance of parties meant that decisions made by the executive would, in most cases, be approved by parliament. Nevertheless, power and policy making were still within the parliamentary arena. In the post-war period policy making has moved outside of the parliamentary arena. It is no longer true that decisions are made exclusively within the process of parliamentary democracy. Party discipline has greatly reduced the freedom of the House of Commons. Yet, in a world that is increasingly complex and where a vast array of information is necessary in order to make policy, government needs support in order to make policy effectively. Instead of using parliament as the institutional foundation for policy making, it is argued that government has increasingly used pressure groups to make policy. Britain is now a 'post-parliamentary democracy'.[1] Government has created a number of integrated and closed relationships with pressure groups and it is these 'networks' that are now the basis of policy making in modern Britain.

DEFINING PRESSURE GROUPS

Pressure groups are organisations that seek to represent the interests of particular sections of society in order to influence public policy. Pressure groups are distinguished from political parties in that they do not usually seek election to office. However, it is sometimes the case that the relationship between pressure groups and parties is extremely close. For example, the green movement sees standing at elections as a means of raising its profile, influencing the political agenda and putting pressure on government. Likewise, the trade union movement created the Labour Party as a means of representing its interests politically. Consequently, there can be very close connections between interest groups and political parties.

It is important to distinguish organisations that try to influence public policy from groups whose primary aim is to represent specific interests in order to influence policy. Most large organisations now try to influence or lobby decision makers. However, if a firm is involved in pressurising a public authority, this is not its primary aim. A pressure group's sole, or main, activity is the representation of a number of individuals or organisations to public authorities. Pressure groups are usually concerned with representing specific interests, such as workers, consumers, finance, or causes, such as the environment, women's rights, anti-abortion. However, there has been, in recent years, a growth of lobbying organisations which offer their services to groups or individuals with the specific purpose of lobbying government.

There are, then, a wide range of pressure groups of different sizes, types and tactics that attempt to influence public authorities over a range of policy matters. In order to understand the role and nature of interest groups it is necessary to characterise pressure groups.

TYPES. TACTICS. EFFECTIVENESS. SUCCESS.

CHARACTERISING PRESSURE GROUPS

There are a range of ways of characterising pressure groups in Britain. Traditionally, pressure groups have been divided into sectoral and cause groups or economic and non-economic groups. Sectoral groups are interest groups[2] that represent a specific sector of the population which has, in some way, a shared set of interests resulting from a particular social attribute. For example, workers in coal mining share interests as coal miners and are represented by a sectional interest group, the National Union of Mineworkers (NUM). The same is true of doctors, farmers and old-aged pensioners.

Cause groups exist to influence policy in favour of specific causes, such as the environment or anti-abortion. These groups can be divided into those with a specific goal, such as reducing the legal age of homosexual sexual activity to 16, and those who are attempting to lobby on policy in general, such as environmental groups. In the case of cause groups, anyone can be a member (as long as they support the cause), whereas for sectional groups it is usually necessary to be a member of the specific group in society to join the interest group.

The problem with the distinction between cause and sectional groups is that the differences are not always clear. It is often the case that many cause groups represent the interests of sectional groups. So, for example, the group lobbying for the reduction in the age of consent for homosexual sex represents a number of sectional groups created to support the rights of gays. Frequently, sectional groups support specific causes and are crucial in the development of cause groups. Medical groups and trade unions provide much of the funding for the various pro-abortion lobbies. It is not always easy to separate cause and sectional groups.

The division between economic and non-economic interest seems to be much clearer. Economic groups represent economic interests, such as business, trade unions, farmers. Non-economic groups represent interests which are not primarily economic: pro- and anti-abortion, gay rights, women's rights. Yet, it is not clear that these distinctions are easy to make. Environmental groups, women's groups and peace groups are not primarily demanding economic goals or representing economic interests but each of these groups has major economic implications and therefore the distinction does little to help us understand the role and impact of interest groups.

These categorisations of interest groups fail in the most important task: helping to understand the influence that groups have on public policy. Wyn Grant has perhaps made the most useful characterisation of pressure groups in distinguishing between insider and outsider groups. For Grant:

> Insider groups are regarded as legitimate by Government and are consulted on a regular basis. Outsider groups either do not wish to become enmeshed in a consultative relationship with officials, or are unable.[3]

Grant distinguishes a range of insider and outsider groups. There are high-profile insiders who use their close relations with government to cultivate important external relations. This is a category that increasingly applies to the BMA which represents doctors. Low-profile insider groups work simply by using internal contacts with government and try to avoid any publicity. Prisoner groups are groups whose existence depends on government. If they wish to retain funding they have therefore to remain insiders and are limited in the criticisms of policy that they can make. One example of a prisoner group is the National Consumers Council (NCC).

There are also a range of outsider groups. Potential insider groups are outsider groups which aim to become insider groups. Many pressure groups start as outsiders unknown or ignored by Whitehall and try to build up contacts through media attention in order to become accepted by government. Outsider groups by necessity are groups that, despite various attempts, cannot achieve access to government. They may not have the ability to make contacts with government or government may not regard them as worth consulting. Ideological outsider groups may believe that the problem they face is a product of the political system and therefore that they will not achieve any change by engaging with the system because it needs to be overthrown. The anarchist group, Class War, is an example. Alternatively, they believe that involvement in the political system will involve compromising the group's political principles and they are not prepared to sacrifice principle for consultation. Green groups are often examples of this type of ideological outsider. They believe that being insiders involves too much compromise and therefore the watering down of their goals. Indeed, the issue of the need to compromise has split the British green movement.

THE IMPACT OF INSIDER STATUS

Achieving insider status for pressure groups can be difficult because it means that they have to be prepared to play by the 'rules of the game'. Abiding by the rules of the game means accepting the government's terms. The rules of the game dictate that only certain behaviour is acceptable: groups that use unlawful methods, make demands that are ideologically opposed to the government, reveal the detail of the process of negotiation with civil servants, or criticise too severely government policy, will be deemed to have broken the rules and could therefore lose insider status.

Why do groups want insider status if it involves such sacrifices? Insider status provides interest groups with a number of compensations:
● They receive government papers and information. They are informed early on of any intended changes in policy.
● They often be given the opportunity to consult with government over proposed changes in policy.
● In the case of some groups with very good insider status, such as teachers in education, doctors in health policy, business in industrial policy and farmers in agricultural policy, insider status can involve

groups in the day-to-day making and implementation of policy. Many insider groups are continually consulted about developments in policy and ways of implementing it. For example, in agricultural policy – at least before Britain joined the European Community (EC) – farmers were involved in a long process of negotiation concerning the setting of agricultural prices. They were also greatly involved in setting the technical regulations which were applied to agriculture.

● Insider groups are accepted on to advisory committees within government and nominated for advisory committees in Europe.

● Some insider groups receive government funding.

Being an insider group is probably the most effective way of influencing government policy. Insiders groups are often involved in the development of policy at a very early stage and therefore may influence policy before it is set in stone. Most outsider groups can only protest once they know of a policy and governments rarely change policy once they have committed themselves. It is easy for government to ignore outsider groups because they can be presented as extreme or as representing a minority. If a pressure group is to influence government on a continual basis it has to become an insider.

For groups to become insiders they need to have something that they can offer to government. There are a range of resources that pressure groups can offer in return for insider status:

● **Information** Government cannot know everything. It often relies on pressure groups to provide the necessary information for developing the detail of policy. It would be impossible to make health policy without the professional knowledge of doctors or to make nuclear policy without the knowledge of nuclear scientists. That said, government will only recognise the information of groups who work within the rules of the game. The information provided by British Nuclear Fuels Ltd on radiation is seen as science whilst that provided by Greenpeace is seen as propaganda.

● **Authority** The authority of governments derives mostly from elections. However, there are obvious deficiencies in electoral authority. Governments are not always elected by a majority, they frequently introduce policies that are not in manifestoes, and authority wanes between elections. Therefore, the support of pressure groups can be used as an alternative source of authority when governments are developing new policies.

● **Simplicity** By having a known set of insider groups within a particular policy area governed by rules of the game, policy making becomes much simpler. Making policy with well-established insiders means that the range of problems and solutions that are likely to come up will be limited. Consequently, an element of surprise is removed from the policy process and this is likely to reduce the difficulties of government.

● **Implementation** Certain groups are necessary for the implementation of policy. Government cannot implement health policy without doctors or agricultural policy without farmers. It is often pressure groups that provide the organisational structure for the implementation of government policy. The only alternatives are to create complicated administrative structures, or to use coercion, both of which produce less than satisfactory results. Government will therefore give insider status in return for support in implementation.

● **Success** To some extent the success of government depends on the activities of groups and organisations in society. This applies particularly to economic groups. In the 1970s, the success of government economic policy depended on trade unions accepting incomes policy. More generally, the government is dependent on the success of business. If business is prosperous, the economy is likely to grow and this will increase the perception that government is successful. Therefore, business is frequently privileged as an interest group. Government has to ensure that business is successful and is more likely to be sympathetic to its interests.

● **Compliance** If government involves an interest group in the development of policy, it can then use the interest group to ensure that its members comply with the policy. This, again, assists government in the development of policy. Frequently, interest groups are involved in ensuring compliance. In particular, professional groups are often left to ensure the regulation of their profession. In the 1960s and 1970s, the Trades Union Congress (TUC) was involved in ensuring that unions complied with incomes policy.

It is clear from these criteria that certain groups are advantaged in gaining insider status. Professional groups, for example, frequently have specialised knowledge that is unavailable to other groups and often society is dependent on these professional groups for the delivery of particular services. It is difficult for government to make policy in these areas without including certain groups in the policy process.

Similarly, business groups have a number of distinct advantages. They are high in status, operate within the context of the dominant values of society and they are important for the economy. They more or less automatically abide by the rules of the game and, therefore, are provided with access on request. There are very few directors in large companies who would be refused access to government. Whether groups are insiders or outsiders, how they behave and their policy impact frequently depend on their resources.

RESOURCES

The resources of pressure groups vary widely. Business groups, for example, usually have a high degree of wealth which means that they can employ good leaders and support systems. They have access to high levels of information and they can provide finance for further research. They can employ lawyers, they can afford to finance lobbying in London and Brussels, they frequently have ready-made organisations, and it is much easier to develop groups because there are relatively few actors with shared interests.

If we consider groups such as consumers, environmentalists or pensioners, it is clear that they have many fewer resources than business. Often they lack finance and cannot develop large organisations or pay salaries for full-time staff. They are frequently dependent on others for information and cannot afford to fund a permanent office in Brussels or London. Whilst a business like ICI will have a permanent office in Brussels monitoring European Union (EU) legislation, contacting other groups and lobbying European institutions, a group such as Consumers in the European Community Group has only one person to represent it on all European committees and to watch all EU proposals and legislation.

It is also much more difficult for groups such as consumers or pensioners to organise. People rarely see themselves primarily as consumers or as pensioners. Consequently, most consumers or pensioners do not think of joining a pressure group. In addition, it is rare that people meet collectively as consumers or pensioners and, as a result, it is very difficult for consumer groups to organise members.

There is also what Olson calls a collective action problem.[4] The costs of joining a pressure group are quite high in terms of time and money whilst the benefits of joining a consumer group are often low. In addition, if a consumer group is successful everyone will benefit whether they are a member or not, and so it is rational to be a 'free rider', thereby gaining benefits without paying the costs of participating.

Membership density.

As a result, the density of membership of consumer groups is much lower than that of business groups. Of the potential 55 million members of consumer groups in this country, membership is little over three million. Conversely, in the Chemical Industries Association all large chemical groups are members, which means a density of 100 per cent. Consequently, the government can, and does, dismiss the demands of consumer groups as not representative of all consumers.

TACTICS

This maldistribution of resources means that pressure groups are forced into using a range of tactics. The actual tactics employed depends on three factors: resources, points of access and degree of preference intensity. Pressure groups are more likely to take high cost action if they feel strongly about an issue.[5]

Direct Press at Govt.
Media

Whether a pressure group is an insider or an outsider, and the resources available to it, will influence where it directs its pressure. Outsider groups, by definition, do not have access to government or the civil service. They tend to direct pressure towards the public and the media. Usually, the goal of outsider groups is to raise public awareness and to get issues on to the political agenda. Frequently, outsider groups attempt to attract media attention by direct action.

Direct Action
Greenpeace raised the issue of the leaking of nuclear waste by illegally blocking the drainage pipe from Sellafield nuclear reactor. Opponents of the extension of the M27 through Twyford Down physically blocked the progress of contractors, albeit unsuccessfully.

Publicity

However, outsider groups do not rely solely on illegal activities to raise the profile of an issue. Often they simply attract media attention to a particular problem. Greenpeace and FoE have been very active in making the public aware of the degree of pollution on British beaches merely by taking water samples and making the results public.

Courts.

Outsider groups, despite not having access to government, frequently use the courts both in Britain and Europe to force government to take action. Greenpeace and Lancashire County Council attempted to block the Thorp nuclear plant by making an application to the High Court on the grounds that the government had acted 'unreasonably and irrationally' by approving Thorp without holding a public inquiry. Despite the failure of the application, Greenpeace did not have to pay costs. The judge felt that, although the government had not acted illegally, there was some justice in the demand for a public inquiry because of the degree of public interest. Environmental groups have also been active, and more successful, in taking the government to the European Court of Justice (ECJ) over implementation of water pollution regulations.

A second access point is parliament. As parliament has less influence over decision making and policy, pressure groups pay less attention to it. However, parliament can be useful in a number of ways. MPs can ensure that particular issues are placed on the political agenda. The issue of rights for the disabled has received much attention because of parliamentary activity. Sometimes, pressure groups use MPs as a way of amending legislation, particularly if the amendment is relatively minor. Occasionally, a well-organised lobbying effort on parliament can actually defeat government. In 1986, the 'Keep Sunday Special' campaign was able to galvanise parliament sufficiently to defeat the second Thatcher government's Shops Bill. Similarly, in 1992, the Major government was forced to rethink its coal mine closure programme following intensive lobbying of MPs.

Perhaps the greatest role for parliament in relation to pressure groups is in the sphere of social issues. Some of the key social measures legislated since the 1960s have been the result of private members' bills on which MPs have been allowed a free vote. Such bills often provide an important opportunity for pressure groups to influence the content of legislation. Abolition of capital punishment, legalisation of abortion and of homosexuality all resulted from private members' bills. Pressure groups play a central role in persuading MPs to adopt issues for such bills, and they are involved in intense campaigns to persuade MPs to pass or oppose legislation. Pressure groups are crucial in these social spheres. They provide the agenda and information for public debate, and can act as a secretariat to MPs who lack the organisational support of ministers and thus rely on pressure groups to provide support and information, and to build the coalition required to enact a bill.

The most important point of access in the British political system is central government. Britain's unitary system of government, strong party discipline and the principle of parliamentary sovereignty mean that power is concentrated largely in Whitehall. If pressure groups are to influence policy making on a continuous basis they need access to government departments, civil servants, and even the prime minister. But, as was noted above, this degree of access is only available to certain groups and, if involvement is to be long term, they have to offer resources to government in return for a place in the policy process.

Nevertheless, pressure groups are extremely important to the British system of government. Richardson and Jordan have argued that the 'British style' of policy making is one of negotiation and consultation.[6] British civil servants seek to avoid conflict and problems. They are prepared to negotiate widely in policy development in order to avoid problems at a later date. Departments have contacts with many groups that they are prepared to consult on a range of issues.[7]

Very few groups automatically have access to the prime minister. Those groups that do tend to be either extremely important for the running of the state or groups or issues of particular interest to the prime minister. The importance of the City of London to the British economy means that it has access to the prime minister through the Bank of England. In the 1960s and 1970s, the prime minister was frequently in contact with the key economic interest groups, such as the TUC and the Confederation of British Industry (CBI), in order to ensure compliance with economic and incomes policies.

Thatcher often established close relationships with individuals in business, such as Lord King of British Airways, and business groups that supported her agenda, such as the Institute of Directors (IoD).[8] She was also very open to think tanks, such as the Adam Smith Institute, the Institute of Economic Affairs and the Centre for Policy Studies. John Major demonstrated a willingness to consider gay rights by meeting the actor Ian McKellen.

An increasingly important target for pressure group attention is the EU, as will be seen in a later chapter. So much legislation now comes from the EU that it is difficult for pressure groups not to campaign at the European level. Again, this arena is only open to groups that can afford to travel to, and operate in, Europe.

STRATEGIES

Dunleavy argues that group strategies depend on their intensity preferences. Groups will take higher cost action when they have stronger feelings on a particular issue. Thus strategies can range from low-cost to high-cost actions:

Low-cost actions
▲ Responding to routine consultation
│ Petitions
│ Lobbying elected representatives
│ Mass media publicity
│ Testifying before legislature
│ Commissioning research
│ Continuous involvement in consultation
│ Public campaigns
│ Demonstrations
│ Attempts to obstruct policy implementation
│ Non-cooperation with government
│ Boycotts or non-compliance
│ Strikes
▼ Civil disobedience
High-cost actions

Source Dunleavy[9]

However, strategies adopted by pressure groups do not necessarily depend solely on preference intensities but also on the resources and status of groups. Groups such as Class Action are likely to embark on civil disobedience campaigns whatever the intensity of their preferences. By contrast, groups that have the option will be involved in continuous consultation, but this is a tactic that is unavailable to many groups. Groups will use a range of strategies simultaneously. They might write to MPs, demonstrate and organise a petition in order to influence government.

Certain groups do not have to do anything to influence government. Groups do not always influence government through observable behaviour such as demonstrations, consultation or boycotts. Powerful economic groups are so important that governments take account of their interests without the groups having to act. Government frequently tailors economic policy to City interests because of the impact City criticism can have on the economy. Groups can also be influential if their ideological preferences match those of government. Finally, the way policy is made influences policy. Post-war agricultural policy was made on the assumption that it was good to increase production. Therefore, a process of agricultural policy making was developed on this premise. No other goals – such as ensuring economic efficiency, protecting the environment, or safeguarding consumer interests – were considered. The interests of non-farm groups were automatically excluded from the policy agenda.

THE INFLUENCE OF PRESSURE GROUPS

The influence of pressure groups depends, to an extent, on their resources, tactics and relationship with government. However, in understanding pressure groups it is important to place them in context. The groups that are important and the resources that influence government change. Who is perceived as influential or important affects resources and affects the impact of a group on government.

Pressure group studies sometimes forget that, in determining the outcomes of policy, it is important to examine the role of government and the interest of state actors as well as pressure groups. Interest groups are just one of the actors involved in the policy-making process and it is important to understand the power relations that exist between groups and government. It is also important to distinguish between groups taking certain actions and their influence on policy. Pressure groups may be involved in consultation with government but that does not mean that they have influence.

NOTES

1 J J Richardson and A.G. Jordan, *Governing Under Pressure* (Martin Robertson, Oxford, 1979).
2 I have not used the term 'interest group' with any specific definition in mind and it will be used interchangably with pressure group.
3 W Grant, *Pressure Groups, Politics and Democracy in Britain* (Philip Allen, London, 1989).
4 M Olson, *The Logic of Collective Action* (Harvard University Press, Cambridge Mass., 1965).
5 P Dunleavy, *Democracy, Bureaucracy and Public Choice* (Harvester Wheatsheaf, Hemel Hempstead, 1991).
6 A G Jordan and J J Richardson, 'The British policy style or the logic of negotiation' in J J Richardson (ed), *Policy Styles in Western Europe* (George Allen and Unwin, London, 1982).
7 A G Jordan and J J Richardson, *Government and Pressure Groups in Britain* (Oxford University Press, Oxford, 1987).
8 W Grant, *Business and Politics in Britain* (Macmillan, London, 1987).
9 Dunleavy, op cit., p.20.

2 CONCEPTUALISING GOVERNMENT/GROUP RELATIONS

To understand the role of pressure groups in the political system, it is necessary to develop a conceptualisation of group influence. Pressure groups are important to political scientists because of the impact they have on policy outcomes. The central interest in pressure groups is on the power relations that exist between government and groups. There are a range of theoretical traditions which conceptualise power relationships between the state and groups. This chapter will outline three main approaches, pluralism, corporatism and policy networks, and highlight their understandings of government/group relations.

PLURALISM

For pluralists, power in modern liberal democracies is widely dispersed. No single group or organisation is able to dominate the political system. A group which is dominant in one policy area will not be dominant in another. A group which wins on one issue will not be successful on another. Pluralists see modern society as a process of continual conflict between groups and between groups and government over policy and resources. No group is continually successful or able to dominate the political system. There is no ruling class or elite but a myriad of groups and organisations moving in and out of the political system attempting to influence government. Government itself is receptive to the pressure of groups. Hence, the political system is fragmented and complex, making it difficult to identify winners and losers. Who exercises power will depend on the policy area and the particular issue.

Pluralism has been the dominant approach in understanding pressure groups and their relations with government. For pluralists, groups are extremely important. They recognise that the formal political system of elections and accountability provides only limited democracy. Therefore, groups are a necessary mechanism for representing the grievances of groups to government. For pluralists, we are all members of various social groups, being workers, consumers, pensioners, residents, parents and so on. Groups will only mobilise when their interests are threatened. Residents in parts of Kent, for example, organised a campaign against the Channel Tunnel rail link when they thought that their houses would be hit by planning blight or their local environment threatened.

Pluralists do not see all pressure groups as equal. They do not deny that some groups have more resources than other. Business groups have better financial resources, ready-made organisations, experienced leaders and economic influence and, therefore, are better resourced than groups representing consumers or pensioners. Nevertheless, pluralists believe that there are checks in the political system which prevent well-resourced groups becoming too powerful:

● If a group organises in a particular area to support a set of interests then countervailing groups will form in order to represent alternative interests. We can see in a range of policy areas that the development of one group leads to the development of a countergroup. The CBI was developed in response to what was seen as the growing power of the TUC. When groups started to lobby for the reform of abortion law, anti-abortion groups, such as Life and the Society for the Protection of the Unborn Child, quickly developed.

● People have overlapping membership of groups. They are consumers and workers, parents and residents. Therefore, it is rarely the case that one group will want completely to dominate another group because some of its members will be in that group.

● Although groups have unequal resources, it may be that a group lacking a particular resource may have a surplus in another. Consumers or pensioners may lack finance and good organisation but are well resourced in terms of votes and the ability to raise media attention. Groups lacking in resources must resort to different tactics.

● Government will ensure that the interests of weakly-resourced groups are given a fair hearing. Government is concerned to gain re-election and will therefore ensure that groups that are not well organised have access to Whitehall. Pluralists recognise that certain pressure groups do develop very close, or clientelistic, relations with departments. However, these departments do not necessarily dominate the policy process, because pluralists argue that there is 'Whitehall pluralism'. Graham Wilson has suggested that even in the case of agricultural policy, where the relationship between the Ministry of Agriculture, Fisheries and Food (MAFF) and the farmers has been very close, pluralism is maintained.[1] In Britain, policy is made through cabinet and cabinet committees and the interests of other groups are represented within these forums. The Treasury attempts to ensure that agricultural policy does not impose too great a burden on the tax-payer. The Department of Trade and Industry seeks to ensure that agricultural policy does not disadvantage the interests of industrialists or damage foreign trade. The Department of the Environment (DoE) attempts to protect the environment from certain agricultural policies.

● Most interest groups are only concerned about a limited range of policy areas. Groups will not dominate the whole of the political system because they are not interested in most policy areas or issues. Health policy, consumer policy, agricultural policy, taxation policy all involve a very different range of pressure groups.

● Government is constrained by the fact that there is a vast array of 'potential groups'. If the interests of these groups are threatened they will organise and the government will be forced to take action. Therefore, the government will ensure that policy does not threaten too greatly the interests of potential groups.

Pluralists do not deny that there are large inequalities in pressure group resources. They maintain that features within the political system ensure that no group dominates the policy process. For pluralists, government is relatively open to group pressures. Groups are important for providing information, legitimacy, assistance with implementation and political support. Therefore, they have access to government, which responds to the various pressures made upon it and usually takes decisions which satisfy the greatest number of groups.

For pluralists, no general rules can be made about which groups are likely succeed. The success of a group will depend on circumstances in a particular policy area. Hewitt, in his study of policy-making in Britain, selected a number of issues in four policy areas: foreign, economic, welfare and social. He examined which groups were involved and which were successful in each issue. He concluded that, 'Very few organisations were involved "significantly" in more than one issue.' In fact, 'conflicting interests are involved in many policy issues without any one interest being consistently successful in achieving its goals.'[2]

PROBLEMS WITH PLURALISM

There are a number of problems with the pluralist analysis. To begin with, it pays too much attention to groups. Pressure groups are clearly extremely important in understanding modern politics. But there is a tendency for pluralists to place too much emphasis on groups, making them the key focus of analysis in understanding politics. It is, however, important to recognise that groups are only part of the equation in understanding how policy is made. Government has tremendous resources and can ignore the pressure of groups. The Thatcher government imposed the poll tax, despite the fact that most of the groups it consulted were opposed to the new tax. It imposed reform on the NHS, despite the opposition of the key medical pressure groups. John Gummer recently said that of the 42,500 individual responses to the latest round of consultation on the need for the Thorp nuclear reprocessing plant, 63 per cent were opposed to the plant but this had raised no issues 'which would cause us to conclude that further consultation or debate is necessary' and the Government announced that it was going ahead with the plant. In understanding policy, it is important to realise that politicians and civil servants have interests that are independent of those of groups and that they can have a very great influence on political outcomes.

The pluralist analysis also exaggerates ease of access. It assumes that if a group tries hard enough over a long period of time, it will achieve access to the political process. However, as was shown in Chapter 1, it is clear that certain groups are regarded as illegitimate and the 'rules of the game' define them as outsiders. Consequently, even in modern democracies, certain groups can have a great deal of difficulty in achieving access to the policy process. Environmental groups and anti-nuclear groups, despite years of protest, have been continuously excluded from nuclear power decision making.

In addition, pluralists concentrate only on observable behaviour. In trying to understand pressure groups, they are concerned with which groups are involved, which policies they support and who is successful. However, some of the most interesting questions in political science cannot be easily observed. In some ways, when analysing power, it is not who is involved in the decision-making process that is important but who is excluded. Often this exclusion is the result of unobservable phenomena such as the 'rules of the game' and the ideology of policy makers. Groups that do not play by rules established by government or that are ideologically opposed to government are unlikely to have access to the policy process.

This concentration on observable behaviour leads pluralists to confuse consultation with influence. If a pressure group is consulted on a policy and the government chooses a policy which the group supports, pluralists see this as an example of the group being influential. However, the government may have made the decision anyway. To understand policy outcomes it is necessary to concentrate on more than the observable behaviour of groups. It is important to understand the context in which decisions are made, the institutions involved in policy making, and the goals and ideology of policy makers.

A further problem is that the concept of Whitehall pluralism is questionable. Most policy is made within departments and, therefore, other departments do not have the opportunity to represent other interests. Moreover, even when issues do go to cabinet or cabinet committee, ministers are frequently too busy to read the papers of other departments and cannot, therefore, offer constructive alternatives. They are also wary of criticising colleagues when they may want their support at a later date.

Finally, professional and economic groups have advantages not available to other groups. It is clear that professional groups, through their control of particular types of knowledge, and economic groups, because of their importance to the economy, have advantages that are unavailable to others.

In the 1950s and 1960s, pluralism was dominant in explaining how pressure groups work and, more generally, how the political system, particularly in the United States, functions. However, it was undermined by a series of events. The student movement, which started off as anti-Vietnam war protest in the United States, spread to Europe. The development of these radical groups suggested that access to the political system was not very open. Moreover, these groups highlighted the continuation of huge inequalities in western liberal democracies and the fact that power was not widely dispersed. There was also increasing recognition that in a number of policy areas governments and groups were developing closed and integrated relationships. It was suggested that the theory which best defined government/group relationships was corporatism rather than pluralism.

CORPORATISM

Corporatists reject the idea that the political system is like a market with groups moving in and out of the political process. Corporatism sees particular groups in a limited range of, usually economic, policy areas developing very close relationships with government and becoming intimately involved in the policy process. A formal model of corporatism has the following features:

● Organised interests representing functional interests show a tendency towards a monopoly position.

● Certain functional interests are granted privileged access to the state's authoritative decision-making processes and are in other ways supported by the state. Such 'licensing' is granted on the basis of adherence to certain norms.

● Membership of such associations may cease to be wholly voluntary, while the associations' privileged monopoly position deprives the members of effective alternative channels.

● In addition to performing a representative function, interest associations also perform a regulatory function over their members on behalf of the state.

● Interest associations and state agencies show increasing bureaucratic tendencies with the result that sectors of society tend to be regulated through hierarchical structures.

● Functional interest associations and state agencies enter into a closed process of bargaining over public policy whereby consciously or not the associations do not fully pursue their immediate advantages but act in a 'system-regarding manner'.[4]

This theory of corporatism maintains that key interest groups are functional groups representing particular sectors in the economy and society, such as teachers, business, miners, engineers, doctors and so on. Each of these groups has a tendency towards monopoly such that there will be one group representing doctors, one engineers and so on. These groups, or a number of them, are given access to decision-making processes if they abide by certain norms or rules of the game, for example, foregoing the right to strike or to make explicit protests about government policy. These associations normally maintain compulsory membership either through sanctions, such as the closed shop, or by depriving individuals of other forms of representation.

In addition to representing members, interest groups also perform a regulatory role. If a trade union, for example, is in a corporatist relationship with government and agrees an incomes policy, it will seek to ensure that its members abide by the policy. For corporatists, it is the group that defines who their members are and what their interest will be, rather than individuals developing groups to represent their interests. Both state agencies and interest groups operate in a hierarchical and bureaucratic manner whereby policy is made by negotiation, through formal committees. It is the leaders of the associations who are involved in decision making. They have little consultation with their members. Once they are involved in this bargaining process, the main concern of the interests frequently becomes simply maintaining the system, and their privileged position, rather than advancing the interests of their members.

The basis of corporatism is that a limited number of groups has a monopoly of representation over a specific interest. This monopoly means that they can be useful to government in the development and implementation of policy. The group controls all the people in a particular sector and can therefore impose government policy on them. In return for this assistance in implementation, the government ensures them a role in the decision-making process.

In the 1960s and 1970s, both Labour and Conservative governments negotiated incomes policies with the TUC and the CBI and expected both partners to ensure that their members abided by the policy and disciplined members who attempted to undermine it. A range of corporatist relationships appeared to be developing in Britain. Trade unions and business were closely involved in incomes, industrial and training policy.

But corporatism was much more widespread than industrial and economic interest groups. It has been argued that a whole range of groups, particularly professional ones, was involved in self-regulation. Groups such as doctors and veterinary surgeons were responsible for setting professional standards and for ensuring that their members abided by the rules. Despite the apparent growth of such relationships, there are a number of criticisms of corporatism.

PROBLEMS WITH CORPORATISM

Corporatism is highly problematic as a theory for understanding government/group relations in Britain, not least because the model often offers a poor analysis of the British political system. It is, for example, questionable whether corporatist relationships were successful. In areas within which business groups and trade unions developed close links with government, there is little evidence that either had much influence on government policy. In the early 1960s, the

National Economic Development Council (NEDC) was created as a forum for economic policy development and brought together trade unions, employers and government to discuss the problems of the British economy. However, NEDC discussions had very little impact on government economic policy.

Corporatist relationships were also frequently unstable. The closest Britain ever came to corporatism was probably in the area of incomes policy in the 1960s and 1970s. However, it was extremely unstable and usually broke down very quickly.

In addition, groups seldom had a monopoly of membership. Only a few professional groups, such as the Royal College of Surgeons, have ever had such a monopoly. Indeed, the peak economic organisations in Britain, the CBI and the TUC, have always been internally weak. In each case, individual members have been stronger than the peak organisation itself. In consequence, each finds it very difficult to impose sanctions on its members. The peak associations had little to offer government in return for a role in decision making.

A further problem is that definitions of corporatism are not very precise. There is a tendency to apply the label corporatism to a wide range of very different relationships. Frequently, it is used to characterise any close relationship between government and an interest group, whether it be interventionist, bilateral or purely consultative.

A final problem is that corporatism has great difficulty in explaining government/interest group relations in Britain in the post-1979 period. Central to corporatist theory is the idea that modern industrial economies are characterised by an inexorable shift towards corporatist relationships. However, the Thatcher governments undermined or abolished many corporatist bodies in Britain. Thatcher immediately excluded the CBI and the TUC from discussions of economic policy. Bodies such as the Manpower Services Commission (MSC) and the NEDC were given a smaller role in policy making. Each of these bodies was eventually abolished.

Neither pluralism nor corporatism can provide a completely satisfactory explanation of the role of groups in the policy process. An alternative approach which uses some of the insights of both pluralism and corporatism is the concept of policy networks.

POLICY NETWORKS

The concept of policy networks recognises that policy making in modern government is segmented. It is highly specialised, with particular agencies and departments responsible for specific parts of policy.[5] Within distinct segments, limited numbers of pressure groups and government actors are involved in making policy. They tend to create high barriers to entry, making it difficult for other groups to take part in the policy process. What is important about the policy network approach is its flexibility in analysing government/group relations. It highlights the different arrangement and number of policy actors involved in distinct policy areas. In some, policy making is open and pluralistic. In others it is closed and corporatist.

Marsh and Rhodes suggest that there is a continuum of policy networks from very open issue networks to closed-policy communities. In an issue network there are many actors, pressure groups and government agencies. Access is relatively open, with groups moving in and out of the policy process. There is often a high level of conflict over policy goals. In a policy community, the number of pressure group and government actors is limited, membership is stable and agreement over the policy agenda is high. Within a policy community, the relationship is one of dependency. Government and pressure group need each other to develop policy and will often be in conflict not with each other but with other communities and networks.[6]

Marsh and Rhodes have outlined a number of dimensions that determine a network's position on the issue network-policy community continuum. They are as follows:
● **Membership** In a policy community the number of participants is limited to one or two departments and a small number of pressure groups. These pressure groups are likely to be professional or economic. The membership of an issue network is large and can encompass any type of group. Issue networks are more likely to occur in areas of social, consumer, and environmental policy rather than in health or economic policy.
● **Integration** Policy communities are characterised by frequent contact between groups and government, in some cases on a day-to-day basis. They have a high level of continuity of members, values and outcomes over a period of years. There is very little change in the policy agenda and the types of policy solutions that the community comes up with. In a policy community there is usually a shared

ideology between participants. All accept the broad framework of policy and agree on policy goals. In an issue network, contact between groups and government will vary greatly with some groups having very little contact and others perhaps only having contact when a particular issue receives a lot of attention. Here there is little agreement on policy, values or outcomes and all are likely to fluctuate greatly.

● **Resources** In a policy community, actors are likely to have significant resources. By contrast, in an issue network resources are likely to be limited. It is more likely that groups involved in a policy network will be hierarchical and have significant control over their members.

● **Power** In a policy community, power is a positive-sum game. Both government and groups actors are likely to gain from the policy and receive benefits from a close relationship. In an issue network, power is more likely to be a zero-sum game with both winners and losers.[7]

TYPES OF NETWORKS

The clearest example of a policy community is in agriculture. For more than 30 years from 1945, the agricultural policy community consisted of a very limited number of actors, chiefly MAFF and the National Farmers' Union (NFU). Both agreed that the basis of policy should be a high level of production supported by a high level of subsidies. Groups which challenged this agenda, such as consumers and environmentalists, were excluded from the policy community.

Inner-city policy during the 1980s provides a good example of an issue network. The network involved several ministries: the Treasury, the Home Office, the departments of Employment, Education, Social Security, several agencies within the Department of Employment; a number of subnational bodies including different tiers of local government, area health authorities and a range of pressure groups. These various organisations found it very difficult to agree on inner-city policy which resulted in the 'continuing failure of inner-city policy'.[8]

It is apparent from these two examples that policy communities have advantages for government over issue networks:

● They make the policy process predictable by removing unexpected demands from the political system. Within a policy community the political agenda is fixed and certain sets of conclusions about policy are agreed. Therefore, government is less likely to be presented with demands it cannot meet.

● They simplify the policy process by defining and limiting the groups with which government has to consult when making policy.
● They remove conflict from the political system.
● They make it easier for government to implement policy. If it can rely on the help of pressure groups to assist with policy implementation through a policy community, it does not have to build administrative machinery to undertake this task. In this sense, a policy community can increase the power of government by making it easier for it to intervene in areas of policy that otherwise would be very difficult. Without the cooperation of the agricultural or health policy communities, it would be very difficult for government to make either agricultural or health policy as neither can easily be done through bureaucratic organisations.

CONCLUSION

The concept of policy networks provides a flexible way of analysing relations between pressure groups and government. Unlike pluralism and corporatism, policy networks do not provide a single view of government/group relationships. Rather, it is possible to see different policy networks developing in different policy areas. In addition, the concept of policy networks does not characterise government/group relationships as conflictual. Rather, it acknowledges that both can gain from a close relationship. Frequently conflicts do not occur between groups and government or even between groups. Conflict is most likely between networks. The next chapter will examine some of the policy to be networks that have developed in post-war Britain.

NOTES

1 G Wilson, *Special Interests and Policy-making* (John Wiley, London, 1977).
2 CJ Hewitt, 'Elites and the Distribution of Power in British Society' in P Stanworth and A Giddens (eds), *Elites and Power in British Society* (Cambridge University Press, Cambridge, 1975).
3 *Times*, 17 December 1993.
4 P Williamson, *Corporatism in Perspective* (Sage, London, 1989).
5 J J Richardson and A G Jordan, *Governing Under Pressure* (Martin Robertson, Oxford, 1979).
6 D Marsh and R Rhodes (eds), *Policy Networks in British Government* (Oxford University Press, Oxford, 1992).
7 Ibid.
8 R A W Rhodes, *Beyond Westminster and Whitehall* (Allen and Unwin, London 1988), p.359.

3 THE DEVELOPMENT OF POLICY NETWORKS IN THE POST-WAR PERIOD

In the years after World War Two, changes in the nature of the British economy, in the role of government, in the nature of groups and in ideology made it easier for groups to establish policy networks. Increasingly decisions were made in policy networks. This chapter looks first at the features of the post-war British state that contributed to the establishment of policy networks and then at the development of policy networks in agriculture, health and industrial relations policy.

STATE, SOCIETY AND ECONOMY: THE CHANGING ROLE OF PRESSURE GROUPS

In the period before World War Two, and in particular before the 1930s, the relationship between pressure groups and government tended to be pluralistic. There was a high degree of conflict between groups and government over policy goals. It was relatively rare for groups to develop close relationships with the state. There was a belief that government had a limited policy role. Economic and social problems should be solved either by the market – in the case of economic problems – by individuals and their families – in the case of welfare problems – or by charities and voluntary associations where collective provision was necessary – in the case of hospital care for the poor. The role of the state was largely confined to maintaining economic and political order. There was some social provision of insurance and education but it tended to be very limited. Only in the depths of depression was the state enticed into an economic role.

Because policies were not developed in many areas, the state had little need for close contact with pressure groups. If groups wanted to organise to provide their own welfare they could certainly do so, but they could not depend on the state to provide welfare for them. This situation was changed by World War Two. Indeed, the British state was transformed into an 'amazingly efficient war machine'.[1] This transformation had a number of implications for pressure groups:
● Production had to be channelled completely to wartime needs. This substantially increased the resources of pressure groups. In war certain

industries became extremely important and the groups which controlled resources such as food, coal and labour, were very important to government. This greatly strengthened their bargaining position.

● War changed perceptions about what the state could and should do. It became apparent that certain problems could not be resolved by the market or individuals but were best resolved through collective provision organised by the state.

● With this realisation, people and groups came to expect more from the state. If the state could organise for war and provide employment and adequate nutrition in wartime why could it not make similar provision in time of peace?

● The state increasingly relied on groups for assistance in the making and implementation of a whole range of policies. Although the state became much larger during the war, it could not do everything. Therefore, the government relied on groups to carry out a number of policies. Although it controlled labour, it relied greatly on trade union cooperation to make this policy work. Expansion of agricultural production could only be developed with the close cooperation of farmers, and in order to set up a national emergency hospital system the government needed to work with doctors. A range of pressure groups thus became continuously involved with government on a day-to-day basis in the development and implementation of policy.

In effect, the war speeded up changes that were already occurring in British society in the 1930s. In this decade the state took on more of a role in economic and welfare policy and developing closer relationships with pressure groups. The war increased the speed of change. More importantly, it irrevocably changed the nature of British state and society, and had a profound impact on state/group relations.

THE IMPACT OF WORLD WAR TWO ON PRESSURE GROUPS

War affected the relationships between groups and the state for a number of reasons:

● The state was much larger after World War Two than it was before it. Many war-time controls and much acceptance of state intervention continued into the post-war period. For Dunleavy:

> The perpetuation of the system into peacetime was not simply the result of inertial momentum. It also reflected a leap in social learning, a recognition of the value of managed social effort for achieving specific and predictable economic and logistical effects.[2]

During the inter-war depression, the *laissez-faire* state was seen to have failed. War proved that state organisation could achieve important societal goals. It further changed capabilities and attitudes and with the rise of Labour and the development of Keynesianism there was ideological and theoretical support for greater state intervention.

● With a larger administrative state, it was possible to intervene in the society to a much greater extent than before the war. The Labour Party was elected with a commitment to full employment and provision of a comprehensive welfare state. Consequently, both government commitment to intervention and its ability to intervene were much greater than they had been in the pre-war period.

● This commitment to economic intervention and welfare spending became the basis of a post-war consensus that committed both major parties to a welfare state and full employment. Underpinning the consensus was an acceptance by both parties of Keynesianism, which held that governments could create full employment and control inflation by adjusting aggregate economic demand. Unemployment could be reduced by cutting taxation or increasing public expenditure, both of which would increase aggregate economic demand.

● After the war, governments sought to avoid social conflict that had occurred in the inter-war years in the rest of Europe. Middlemas points out that governments used economic pressure groups such as the TUC and CBI (which until the mid-1960s was known as the Federation of British Industry) as institutions for harmonising conflicting interests. Pressure groups thus helped to aggregate demands and to ensure that government did not have to deal with conflict.

● With government playing a greater role in society and increasing pressure-group expectations, groups became better organised and started to increase their membership. Economic groups changed first. In the 1950s and 1960s, as social pressure for government action increased, consumer and environmental groups developed. People expected more from government and therefore demanded more.

These changes created a need for pressure groups and governments to build close relationships. Governments needed pressure groups to avoid conflict. Pressure groups needed governments to meet their social demands. Consequently, it became easier for groups to develop policy networks with government. Three particularly important networks developed in agricultural, health and industrial relations policy.

DEVELOPMENT OF THE AGRICULTURAL POLICY COMMUNITY

Agriculture is probably the best British example of a closed policy community. In the post-war years, the NFU and MAFF developed a very close relationship, with the NFU involved in all aspects of agricultural policy making. Through the Annual Review of agricultural prices it was given institutionalised access to the whole process of setting agricultural subsidies. In addition, the ministry and the union were not usually in conflict but agreed on the goals of agricultural policy which were to increase agricultural productivity and to ensure that prices were set to provide farmers with a reasonable standard of living.

The influence of farmers was not exercised through lobbying, demonstrations or strikes but through their relationship with the ministry. Farmers had not always been in this position, nor was it inevitable that the farming community would develop close relations with government. Indeed, in the inter-war period agricultural policy was made in a very pluralistic arena. Present were a number of groups and departments including farmers, landowners, food manufactures, import companies, the Board of Trade, the Foreign Office and the Colonial Office. The primary concern of policy makers was not prices paid to farmers but maintenance of free trade in food in order to keep food prices low and to ensure trade with colonial countries. Farmers were just one of many groups involved in agricultural policy and they relied on the normal lobbying techniques of pressure groups, such as deputations to ministers, lobbying MPs and holding mass demonstrations.

A series of factors helped to transform a very pluralistic arena into a closed policy community. They include:
● **Fear of war** As soon as war with Germany seemed possible, policy makers sought to prepare agriculture for increased production. Government introduced a number of measures to increase agricultural productivity and gradually also introduced a number of agricultural subsidies. At the time, these policies were seen purely as emergency measures intended to last the duration of the war.
● **Changes in the NFU** The farmers' union realised that the approach of war placed it in a potentially powerful position. Consequently, it made a conscious effort to build its membership, to become the sole farming organisation and to act 'responsibly' within the 'rules of the game'. As a result, when government started to intervene in agriculture, it turned to the NFU for advice.
● **World War Two and its immediate aftermath** Events during and

directly after the war firmly established the agricultural policy community. During the war government had no choice but to increase agricultural production. In order to secure more food it had to promise farmers high prices. Farmers thereby gained a strong position. Government could not afford to lose their confidence and so created the Annual Review of prices which committed it to maintaining farm incomes. Although policy makers did not intend high prices and production to be continued after the war, a combination of world food shortage and lack of dollars with which to buy food imports that forced them to extend the wartime policy. The result was that policy that was increasingly accepted as the only possible option for agriculture.

● **Treasury support for the policy** Because of Britain's shortage of dollars and the need to reduce spending on imports, the Treasury was prepared to support the policy of expanding agricultural production through subsidies, thereby reversing its earlier hostility to agricultural subsidies. Thus, the NFU and the Ministry of Agriculture were allowed to develop agricultural policy without the representation of other interests.[3]

Consequently, the policy which was established to deal with agriculture during a wartime emergency became widely accepted as the only possible policy for agriculture. From the 1950s to the 1970s all parties accepted largely without question the need to increase agricultural production. In addition, the nature of the agricultural policy community meant that other pressure groups which might challenge the NFU were excluded from the policy process. Parliament had little input into agricultural policy making. Other farming groups, such as the Country Landowners Association and the National Union of Agricultural Workers, were largely excluded from the Annual Review. Consumer groups were not consulted by MAFF. Environmentalists were believed to be irrelevant to agricultural policy making.[4]

Agricultural policy in the post-war period did not result from conventional pressure group activity. Rather it was generated by a policy community protected by an ideology of increased production and the institutions of the Ministry of Agriculture and the Annual Review. Groups that were likely to challenge the dominant agenda were excluded. Policy was made by a very small elite group that rarely considered alternative policy options. The issue was never 'should agriculture be supported?' Rather it was 'how much support should farmers receive?' Farmers were not powerful because of their pressure group. The NFU's relationship with the ministry made them strong.

DEVELOPMENT OF THE HEALTH POLICY COMMUNITY

Doctors form another group that is frequently cited as being influential. They clearly have an important resource in terms of their professional knowledge, which means that they possess specialised information unavailable to other groups and a high degree of control over the delivery of their services. Nevertheless, like farmers they are not inherently powerful. Their power derives more from their relationship with the Department of Health (DoH) than from the resources of their pressure groups – the BMA and the Royal Colleges.

As was the case in agriculture, doctors only started to become influential once government took an interest in health policy. In the nineteenth century, doctors were in many ways a poorly-paid proletariat. In the early decades of the twentieth century severe problems with British health care provision prompted governments to increase their interest in health policy. Immediately before World War Two policy makers considered various plans to reform health care provision.

Nevertheless, it was the intervention of war which led government, insurance companies, political parties and doctors to agree that some form of comprehensive health service was necessary. There was at this time a great deal of disagreement between the various groups concerning how this service was to be provided. The wartime coalition government negotiated with the doctors and a range of other interests before producing the 1944 Health White Paper. However, the paper revealed the pluralism of the policy process with no particular group dominating the outcome. In consequence, no group was very happy with the proposed policy. In particular, doctors opposed many elements of it and as a result the policy process was deadlocked.

It took the election of a Labour government in 1945 to break the deadlock. This election changed the political balance. The Labour government had a clear idea of the type of health policy it wanted, its landslide victory gave it a high degree of political authority, and the health minister, Aneurin Bevan, was prepared to use his authority to challenge doctors. He was also prepared to make concessions to allow progress and establish the basis for a health policy consensus.

Bevan did two important things which laid the foundations of the health policy community. First, he nationalised hospitals, placing them under government control and removing voluntary hospitals and local authorities from the policy process. Second, realising that there was important opposition from doctors to Labour's plans, he made a series of concessions designed to bring them into a functioning policy community. He allowed them to continue private practice, he did not make GPs state employees and he related their pay to the number of patients they treated.[5] In addition, he split the profession by offering further concessions to consultants who were released from local authority control, given influence in the administrative structure, and promised a certain number of private beds. The London teaching hospitals were given special status.

It is clear that once government was committed to a National Health Service (NHS), doctors became very powerful because government relied on them for the delivery of health care. In making concessions to doctors, Bevan established the policy community. He excluded a number of actors who had previously been involved in health policy, such as local authorities, charities and insurance companies, and he established a consensus between doctors and government, notably the Ministry of Health, on how the NHS should operate and what the role of doctors within it should be.

The compromise involved in the creation of the NHS made doctors dependent on the state for their income and the state dependent on doctors for the implementation of health policy.[6] This mutual dependence was institutionalised through the health policy community based on a single ministry – the Ministry of Health up to 1968, the Department of Health and Social Security from 1968 to 1988 and the Department of Health from 1988. This single ministry has had an almost total monopoly over health policy, shared with its partners in the community, the BMA and, to a lesser extent, the Royal Colleges.

Like farmers, doctors influence health policy not through traditional pressure group activity but through their very close relationship with government. The health policy community is supported by a consensus that accepts the central importance of a free health service, acknowledges a belief in doctors' clinical autonomy, promotes a high degree of self-regulation by professional associations, tolerates the self-employed status of GPs, and guarantees doctors a central role in the making and administration of health policy. A free health service is seen as generally desirable and so there is no need for anyone other than doctors and ministry officials to be involved in policy making.

At the same time, the ministry recognised from the start that doctors had to be free to make clinical decisions. While the state provided money, doctors determined what treatment was best. The position of doctors in making health policy was therefore strong. Their role was institutionalised at every level of the NHS whilst most other groups, such as nurses, ancillary workers and patients, were excluded from the policy process. Even the role of the Treasury and parliament was limited.[7] Health policy thus provides another example of a highly integrated policy community.

TRADE UNIONS AND GOVERNMENT

The relationship between government and the trade union movement has always been much more complicated than is that with either doctors or farmers. This is so for a number of reasons:
● Trade unions and government have always had an adversarial relationship. Trade unions have consistently seen governments as ignoring their wage demands, causing economic problems and excluding unions from the policy process. Governments have perceived trade unions as confrontational, demanding too much in terms of wages and causing other economic problems.
● Trade unions were for a long time seen as outsiders and it has thus been very difficult for unions to develop close relations with government. In consequence, trade unions have frequently had to use their economic resources, through strikes, as a way of influencing policy.
● Unlike farmers and doctors, who have a limited number of organisations to represent their interests, workers have been divided into hundreds of trade unions who often do not agree amongst themselves. This has made it difficult to reach agreement with government.
● Frequently, the issues which have concerned trade unions, such as wages, employment and the economy, do not affect a small group of society but are a central concern of everyone, including most pressure groups. Therefore, it has been a great deal more difficult to close these policy areas off to a limited range of groups.

Despite these difficulties, relationships between government and the trade union movement gradually became closer during the post-war era in a range of areas including incomes, industrial, economic and training policy. Yet in none of these areas could unions be said to have become involved in a closed policy community. Rather, government/union relations have resembled a much looser policy network.

As was the case with farmers and doctors, close relations between unions and government resulted largely from the events of World War Two. In March 1938, when government began to think seriously about the German threat, the Prime Minister, Neville Chamberlain, met the TUC General Council for the first time since 1926 to explain the government's rearmament programme. In order to prepare for war government needed the support of the trade unions. According to Martin, 'Ministerial moves to secure the support of the unions date from this time, though there was a half-hearted air about these efforts until war actually came.'[8]

In war the unions played a pivotal role in the economy and, therefore, government developed close relations with them in a number of areas. As soon as war started government/union contacts increased greatly and government created the National Joint Advisory Council to represent unions and employers. In the first eight months of war, ten departments 'either created consultative bodies or admitted the unions to existing bodies'.[9] Once Churchill became Prime Minister of the coalition government, unions were highly integrated into all levels of Whitehall. They were represented within 18 departments and their role was no longer confined to industrial issues. War made labour the ultimate resource. Production had to be maintained and the Labour minister, Ernest Bevin, used his position to make the Ministry of Labour the 'principal department of Government'. He also ensured that the trade unions were continuously consulted and involved closely in the development of labour policy. 'Between 1940 and 1945, the trade union movement achieved its fundamental aim of parity with the employers in the eyes of the Government.'[10]

When war ended, the unions continued their consultative role. In the period after the war, the trade unions maintained a close relationship with government, although they did lose some of the influence they had had during the war. In the 1950s, the basis of government links with trade unions was voluntarism. The bargain made between labour, business and government was that government would maintain full employment and trade unions would not present a political challenge to government. Rather they would be left to pursue wage claims with employers free from government intervention. At the same time, governments, both Labour and Conservative, were prepared to consult trade unions over issues which were seen as affecting their interests. This, according to Middlemas, was a period of harmonious relations between government, trade unions and business.

Although the highly-institutionalised relationships of the war were wound down, contacts between government, trade unions and business continued on a formal and informal basis at a very intense level. As Martin notes:

> There was little to distinguish the Conservative Governments of 1951-64 from the Attlee Government so far as their consultative relationship with the TUC was concerned. Ad hoc consultation at all levels of Government remained frequent and, for the most part, free of difficulty. Post-Churchill Government leaders, for example, had many discussions with TUC representatives on major issues relating to the European Economic Community, the European Free Trade Area and the Organization for European Economic Cooperation. Nor does there appear to have been any significant reduction in the range of formal advisory bodies under the Conservatives.

It was accepted by both parties that unions were legitimate organisations that had a role to play in government.

In the 1960s, things started to go wrong for a number of reasons:
● After a period of sustained economic growth, Britain appeared to be suffering from economic problems and was unable to keep up with its main economic competitors.
● Union membership was increasing and workers were expecting pay rises above the rate of inflation.
● These two factors produced an increased militancy amongst trade unionists and there was an increased number of strikes and a growth in the number of wildcat strikes.
● After a period of relative agreement over the direction of economic policy, there was increased politicisation of economic issues. As a result, there was increasing conflict between trade unions, employers and government over economic policy.

Thus, in the 1960s and into the 1970s, the problems of the British economy had the effect of politicising both industrial relations and economic policy. There was increasing conflict between unions, government and employers over wages, and the political parties were becoming increasingly polarised over economic policy. Governments of both parties adopted two strategies to deal with increasingly conflictual government/trade union relations. On the one hand they attempted a strategy of corporatism. This involved setting up formal tripartite institutions to deal with issues of economic and incomes policy. On the other they resorted to legislation.

In the sphere of economic policy, the Macmillan government created the NEDC as a forum within which business, unions and government could meet to discuss the problems of the British economy and policies for solving them. These were extended in the 1970s when government created sectoral working parties, which were intended to conduct intensive examinations of the British economy in order to see how problems of modernisation and productivity could be resolved.

The other major area of corporatism was incomes policy. With governments facing increasing difficulty in controlling inflation in the 1960s, they shifted away from voluntarism and sought to control wages through incomes policy. In order to secure the support of trade unions government created corporatist bodies for the negotiation of policy and the attainment of union support in implementation. The first formal tripartite body for the development of incomes policy was the National Board for Price and Incomes. This was the beginning of a whole range of incomes policies which continued until 1979.

Corporatist strategy was, however, never very successful. Unions, business, and government had difficulty in agreeing a consensual economic policy. Moreover, the tripartite bodies set up to examine economic policy had no executive power. They could not make economic policy. This was under control of the Treasury, which continued to function with little regard to the demands of business and labour.

In addition, incomes policies always failed. Although there were periods when incomes policies limited pay rises for a short time, these were usually followed by a pay explosion. Often, trade unions were not prepared to accept government limits on pay increases, and even when trade union leaders did accept, their members often did not and were prepared to take industrial action to break the agreed pay norm.

Corporatist relations generally failed in Britain because of the decentralised nature of British trade unions. Trade unions tend to be strong at shop-floor level but very weak at central level. Although trade union leaders could reach agreement with government, they could not impose these measures on their members. Consequently, governments of both parties turned to legislation as a mechanism for reducing the power of unions at the shop-floor level.

In 1968, Wilson's Labour government introduced a White Paper, *In Place of Strife,* which proposed legislation intended to reduce the power of the trade unions. The White Paper suggested that government be given the power to intervene in unofficial strikes and inter-union disputes. However, trade unions were not prepared to accept legislative control, especially from a Labour government. The measures were defeated by a coalition of trade unions and Labour MPs.

When the Conservative came to power in 1970, they were committed to introducing trade union legislation. In 1971, the Industrial Relations Act was passed. The Act required all trade unions to register and reduced some of the blanket legal immunities that unions had been granted since 1906. It created a National Industrial Relations Court to which complaints against unions and companies could be taken. It allowed for the secretary of state to apply for a 'cooling off' period before a strike commenced. However, the law failed because companies did not use it and unions refused to register. As they withdrew from all cooperation with government it was politically disastrous.[11] The legislation was repealed by the Labour government in 1974.

Once Labour was returned to power in 1974, there was a great awareness of the need to maintain the support of trade unions and government initially worked very closely with the unions on economic policy. Together they established the Social Contract whereby government agreed to consult with the trade unions on economic issues in return for trade union acceptance of incomes policy. However, the arrangement broke down in the winter of 1978-79.

Thus, in the post-war period, the trade unions and government developed a range of policy networks covering economic and incomes policy. However, these networks were never as closed as those in agriculture and health. This was partly because trade unions could not control their members in the way the other organisations could, and partly because there was a lack of consensus between government and unions, unions and business, and even unions and unions.

CONCLUSION

World War Two changed both the nature and the role of the state. Thus, relationships between government and pressure groups altered. In many areas government established policy networks with pressure groups. In addition to the areas analysed in detail in this chapter, such networks were established in transport, power, pollution control, education and many other policy areas. However, in the 1970s and 1980s things began to change and established policy networks were threatened by economic and political change, the rise of new social movements (NSMs), and Britain's membership of the EC. Each development had major implications for Britain's pressure groups.

NOTES

1 K Middlemas, *Politics in Industrial Society* (Andre Deutsch, London, 1979), p.267.
2 P Dunleavy, 'The Paradox of Ungrounded Statism' in F G Castles, *The History of Comparative Public Policy* (Polity Press, Oxford, 1989), p.278.
3 MJ Smith, *The Politics of Agricultural Support in Britain* (Dartmouth, Aldershot, 1990).
4. P Lowe, G Cox, M McEwan, T O'Riordan and M Winter, *Countryside Conflicts* (Gower, London, 1986).
5 JE Pater, *The Making of the National Health Service* (King Edward's Hospital Fund for London, London, 1981).
6 R Klein, 'The State and the Profession: The Politics of the Double Bed' *British Medical Journal*, 301, 1990, pp.700-2.
7 R Klein, *The Politics of the NHS* (Longman, London, 1989).
8 R Martin, *TUC: The Growth of a Pressure Group 1868-1976* (Claredon Press, Oxford, 1980), p.245.
9 Ibid. p.247.
10 Middlemas, op cit. p.301.
11 D Marsh, *The New Politics of British Trade Unionism* (Macmillan, London, 1992).

4 THE IMPACT OF ECONOMIC AND POLITICAL CHANGE

Particular economic and political conditions at the end of World War Two established the framework for government/group relations in the post-war period. This context led to the creation of a range of relatively closed policy networks in a number of policy areas. The 1970s and 1980s saw important economic and political changes with the restructuring of the British economy and the rise of the New Right. These changes affected the resources and importance of pressure groups and the way in which they were perceived by policy makers. This then affected relationships between government and groups. This chapter investigates the impact of these political and economic changes on groups.

ECONOMIC CHANGE

Britain has undergone profound economic change in the post-war period. However, the British economy went through particularly great readjustment in the 1970s and 1980s with the decline in heavy manufacturing industry, the growth of the service sector, the rise in part-time employment and the introduction of new management and production techniques. This has had an important effect on the resources available to certain groups and their potential impact on government.

The key economic changes which have marked recent decades are:
● **Britain's relative economic decline** Throughout the post-war period, Britain has failed to grow as fast as its competitors. This has had important implications for pressure groups. The basis of policy networks, and of involvement of pressure groups in government, is that, in return for responsible behaviour, government will meet pressure groups' demands. Farmers were promised subsidies, doctors an expanding health service and trade unions rising living standards. However, as the British economy failed to grow as fast as expectations and demands, conflicts developed between government and groups over policies and the level of public expenditure. The tendency of governments, both Labour and Conservative, was to increase expenditure faster than the rate of economic growth. This extravagance

increased the level of taxation and the amount of public borrowing, thereby having adverse effects on both the economy and the sectors of society that felt they were being overburdened with tax. The result was periodic bouts of economic crisis in which government was forced to cut public expenditure. The result was often conflict with public sector organisations and the trade unions.

● **The decline of manufacturing** Britain's economic decline has been simultaneous with a decline in the British manufacturing sector. Between 1946 and 1987 employment in manufacturing declined from 34 per cent to 22 per cent of total employment. However, between 1946 and 1974 manufacturing output grew faster than did the economy as a whole. Since 1974, the growth in manufacturing output has been more or less flat with periods of absolute decline. In particular, the period 1979-83 saw a major relative and absolute decline in manufacturing output and employment.[1] This change has had important implications for many pressure groups, notably the trade unions. Many have lost influence because their industries have declined and are no longer strategically important. The most obvious casualty is the NUM, which has fallen from 750,000 members in 1946 to 30,000 in 1994. As a result, the miners have declined from being a highly effective group to one that is impotent in the face of pit closures. However, it is not only unions that have been affected. Manufacturing industry also feels that its interests have been ignored by government. There has been a long tradition of belief in Britain that government has been more receptive to the interests of the City than to those of manufacturing. In the early period of the Thatcher governments, there was a feeling that the interests of manufacturing were being almost completely excluded from the policy process.

● **The growth of the service sector** Whilst manufacturing industry and employment have declined, there has been a growth in service industries, such as retail, financial services and the leisure industry. In the 1960s, for the first time, more than 50 per cent of the population were employed in the service sector. Since then, service employment has continued to increase. In the period since 1974, when manufacturing output has stagnated, service output has increased by 43.5 per cent.[2] This shift to service employment, it is argued, has changed interests, the relative power of groups and the attitudes and beliefs of people. It is no longer the large economic actors that are dominant in terms of public policy, but new interests that have come into play. Dunleavy and Husbands argue that people's interests have shifted from production issues to consumption issues.[3] Therefore, consumer interests and consumer groups have become increasingly important. At the economic level the interests of retailers and finance have become more significant than those of manufacturing. Because workers in the service sector are less likely to be members of trade unions, this change has further decreased the power of trade unions.

● **Changes in patterns of production** Not only has there been a shift from manufacturing to services, but the way that manufacturing is organised has also changed. The key change is the development of both flexible production and flexible employment. Production has become flexible in that it increasingly takes place in small plants which can more easily be moved from region to region and country to country. It is also more flexible in what it can produce. New technology allows greater differentiation in production prompting smaller production runs and greater product variation. The shift to a flexible workforce has seen the growth of part-time working, particularly amongst women, changes in the pattern of shift-working, the breakdown of demarcation lines, and changes in patterns of payment. Increasingly, especially in the public sector, there is a growing division between those on temporary and those on permanent contracts.[4] The shift to flexible production has also made it much easier for business to avoid national regulation, placing transnational companies in a strong bargaining position with governments. In the early-1980s, Hoover moved from France to Scotland when faced with high labour costs in France. This shift also weakens the position of unions as production units become smaller and workforces become dispersed and temporary, making it more difficult to organise unions. In addition, workers on temporary and part-time contracts are in a very weak position when it comes to taking industrial action.

● **The growth of an information society** Advanced industrial societies have become increasingly dependent on information technology. An expansion of higher education has given more people access to knowledge and has resulted in growing expertise and specialisation. Within a whole range of occupations knowledge has become increasingly specialised, making it difficult for non-experts to hold professions to account. The growth of an information society has had contradictory effects on pressure groups. Through the expansion of education, more people have been provided with the ability and knowledge to challenge traditional centres of power. This growth can, therefore, be seen as partly responsible for the growth of NSMs in areas such as peace and the environment. At the same time, it has made knowledge an important resource which has increased the power of professional groups that are able to monopolise specialised information. Increased complexity and the diversity of sources of knowledge shift power from economic groups to NSMs and professional groups.

Economic change in Britain has, it seems, shifted power from large industrial groups to smaller professional and consumer groups. Power has also shifted from national industrial capital to multi-national financial capital. Class politics has become less important and people are more concerned with their interests as consumers than as producers. The establishment of a well-educated affluent, new middle class has led to the creation of NSMs that are interested in cross-class issues of peace, race, gender and the environment. These new groups have challenged established policy networks. The extent to which this is the case will be examined in later chapters. What cannot be denied is that important social and economic change has occurred in Britain and has had political effects. The most notable is the rise of Thatcherism, which has also been a threat to traditional policy networks.

THE IMPACT OF THATCHERISM ON PRESSURE GROUPS

Thatcherism was partly a response to Britain's economic problems which, according to New Right ideology, were to some extent due to the activities of pressure groups. Its key aims were to reduce the size and role of the state, reduce public expenditure and re-establish a free market economy. Interest groups were seen as a threat to each of these goals. Groups frequently demanded increased state intervention, more public expenditure and, through protecting their own privileges with restricted access and subsidies, distorted the market. Thatcherism offered a distinctive critique of the role of pressure groups in society:

● **Pressure groups and the problem of overload** The New Right believes that pressure groups have presented the state with too many demands and that this has led to state intervention in areas where the state should not intervene. Consequently, the state has had too many problems to deal with and this has led to policy failure. To some extent pressure groups have made modern society ungovernable. As the state has failed to deliver on all policy demands, the authority of the state has declined and this has led to increased challenges to the power of government.[5] A by-product of overload has been the 'crowding out' of the private sector. As government spending on public services has increased, so less money has been available for private investment. Consequently, investment in the private sector has declined, thereby exacerbating Britain's economic decline.

● **Pressure groups as the protection of special interests** The New Right believes that interest groups distort the political process by establishing special relationships (or policy networks) with government. These relationships comprise government and groups working together to expand the nature and cost of public programmes. Bureaucrats and interest groups have a shared interest in ensuring the expansion of public expenditure because of the benefits that accrue to them. Consequently, pressure groups protect their own interests by creating social closure. They use barriers, such as closed shops or professional qualification, to limit access to particular occupations and thus push up the cost of their services. In addition, they demand subsidies and state regulation to protect their privileges and living standards. In each of these ways, interest groups distort the market and prevent economic rationalisation. Olson argues that pressure groups organise in order to reduce the impact of the market on their members.[6] The result is economic stagnation and ultimately economic decline.

● **Britain as a corporate society** For Thatcherites, interest groups have turned Britain into a corporate society, distorting the market and producing economic decline. For the New Right, Britain in the post-war period was becoming an increasingly corporatist society with decisions that should have been made by the market being made by agreement between government and groups. A range of tripartite bodies, such as the NEDC, the MSC and the Wages Council, protected the interests of the producer rather than those of the consumer. In addition, corporatism distorted the democratic process. Decisions that should have been made by parliament were being made by trade unions and employers in consultation with government. For the New Right, the key political relationship should not be between government and groups but between individuals and parliament.

The basis of Thatcherism was an attempt to change the relationship between state and society. The state, it was argued, should be relatively small and not responsible for providing a whole range of social services. For Thatcherism, individuals are more important than groups. Therefore, it was essential to break up what was seen as the corporate society of the 1970s. In order to achieve this goal Conservative governments since 1979 have undertaken a number of measures that have challenged the roles of pressure groups and existing policy networks. These include:

● **Shifting the terms of political debate** After World War Two pressure government/group relations were based on certain conceptions about the role of the state. In order to create and deliver the welfare state it was necessary to develop a range of policy networks. Thatcherism believed that the welfare state should be reduced and, therefore, it had less need for the policy networks of the post-war era. In order to achieve this goal, the Thatcher governments sought to shift the terms of political debate, undermining commitments to a welfare state and promoting the notion of a free-market economy. The Thatcher and Major governments have consistently pursued policies of privatisation and reform of the welfare state in order to shift the political debate away from the post-war social democratic consensus. In some ways these governments have been successful in changing the political agenda. The Labour Party appears to have reconciled itself to a smaller public sector, the need to restrain tax increases and most of the reforms undertaken in health, education and trade unionism. Yet, there is contradictory evidence amongst the wider electorate. Many people still support the social democratic agenda and, despite the Conservatives' electoral success, the majority of people are still committed to the welfare state, public ownership and increased public expenditure.[7] Nevertheless, it may be the case that after 15 years of Conservative government people now expect less from government. In a sense, the Conservatives have resolved the problem of overload as groups are now less likely to demand that government solve problems. With, for example, the privatisation of gas, electricity and water, the issue of price increases in these utilities is no longer a government problem but a problem for the respective industries. Government no longer controls these industries (although in reality there is public control through regulation) and, as a result, problems of price or pollution have to be resolved between producers and consumers.

● **Challenging intermediate institutions** In changing the role of the state and the political agenda, Conservative governments have also changed the types of relationship they have with intermediate bodies, such as pressure groups, universities, churches, and local authorities. For Thatcherism, parliament is sovereign and a government elected with a majority has a mandate to implement its policies. Intermediate institutions – organisations which come between individuals and the state – are held to distort or resist the implementation of government policy. Consequently, Conservative governments have been committed either to their abolition or to reduction of their power. Local authorities, which were believed to be committed to the types of welfare policies that central government was seeking to reform, have

been targeted in this way. Similarly, the government saw local education authorities (LEAs) as obstacles to government education policy
and so allowed schools to opt out of local authority control and
develop direct relationships with the Department for Education.
Perhaps more surprisingly, the Thatcher governments challenged
intermediate institutions such as the church, universities and the BBC
which were perceived as too 'conservative'. These organisations were
either obstacles to the new Thatcherite agenda or resistant to market
forces and so needed to be reformed. According to Andrew Gamble,

> Legitimacy is withdrawn from voluntary associations like trade
> unions and from public institutions like the BBC, the universities and
> state education system, nationalised industries and local Govern-
> ment, until they have reformed themselves or been reformed from
> outside. A whole range of what were seen as corporatist intermedi-
> ate institutions, such as the NEDC, MSC and Wages Council, have
> been abolished by the Thatcher and Major governments.[8]

● **The privileging of new interest groups** Whilst being suspicious of
many interests groups, such as trade unions and even professional
groups associated with the establishment of the welfare state,
Conservative governments have given access to interest groups that
had been partially excluded in the past. In terms of business interests,
rather than relying largely on the CBI for representation of business
interests, the Thatcher governments established close relations with
the more right-wing IoD. It was also very open to the interests of the
City of London and was prepared to listen to its demands on economic policy and on the issue of the deregulation of financial services.
Recent Conservative governments have also been more receptive to
groups held to be in sympathy with New Right ideas, such as the
Freedom Association. In addition, they have attempted to build a
broad base of support amongst the new affluent working class in the
South and the more established middle class. Conservative policies in
the spheres of taxation and home ownership have been intended to
shift resources to these groups.[9] Pressure groups have lost power to
these social groups as individuals. Behind the reforms in education
has been the endeavour to see power move from teachers' unions to
concerned parents who, for Thatcher, perhaps mistakenly, are more
trustworthy educationalists. Power has thus been shifted from LEAs to
schools and their governors, and the role of parent governors has
been increased. In addition, the balance of representation on quasi-
autonomous non-governmental bodies has been changed. Trade
union representation on health authorities has been reduced. School

governors are no longer representatives of political parties but are drawn from the local community. In the past, these bodies tended to have a balance of representatives from unions, business and political parties. Now there is much more likelihood that business people will make up committees. Responsibilities which have traditionally been held by elected councillors are now being handed over to 70,000 'quangocrats'.[10]

● **The new role of think tanks** Conservative governments have changed a number of policy networks. Instead of relying on pressure groups, the government has increasingly relied on think tanks to provide ideas and information for new policies. Think tanks are independent from government but undertake research with the aim of influencing government policy. The past two decades have witnessed the growth of a number of New Right think tanks with the explicit aim of shifting the policy agenda to the right. Bodies such as the Institute of Economic Affairs, the Centre for Policy Studies and the Adam Smith Institute have been at the forefront of political debate in areas such as privatisation, reform of the health service, family policy and educational reform. Think tanks have been very useful for government in terms of kite flying. They have often been prepared to suggest policies which government is worried might be seen as too extreme. In this way, think tanks have been successful at shifting the agenda and winning support for ideas which had previously been seen as too radical. Perhaps one of the clearest examples is the privatisation of prisons. In the early 1980s, government would not have dreamt of proposing such a policy. However, it was suggested by a number of think tanks in the mid-1980s and, in 1993, the first privatised prison, Wold Remand Centre, was established in Hull with relatively little opposition. A similar process occurred with the privatisation of water. Perhaps more importantly, think tanks have become members of new government policy networks, notably in health and education.

● **The role of voluntary associations in the delivery of services** Despite government mistrust of interest groups and the perception that they distort the economic and political process, it has relied on certain groups to take an increased role. As government has changed the nature of the welfare state, it has increasingly turned to voluntary associations – charities – to deliver public services. Government now provides grants to organisations to provide welfare services. Rather than rely on local authorities to provide public housing, government is increasingly turning to housing associations to produce affordable housing for the less well off. Even in areas such as environmental policy, voluntary groups have been used to implement policy. The Scottish

Office has set up and funded UK2000 with the aim of improving the environment through the use of volunteers and employment training programmes. The programme is implemented not by civil servants but by four voluntary bodies – Community Service Volunteers, Scottish Conservation Projects Trust, Scottish Wildlife Trust, and Sustainable Transport – which receive grants from the Scottish Office via UK2000.[11]

● **The increased role of professional lobbyists** An important change that occurred during the 1980s was the growth of professional lobbyists. An increasing number of organisations and pressure groups rely on these lobbyists to inform them of the latest developments within government and to pressure MPs and government on their behalf.

Thatcherism has thus affected the relationship between pressure groups and government in a number of ways. Through reforms of central government, local authorities and the welfare state, it has changed the types of groups which are involved in policy making. In addition, its distinct ideology affects the perception of groups in the policy process and the perception of which groups are important. It has also built new coalitions which by-pass traditional pressure groups and networks. The experience of the past 15 years demonstrates the way in which pressure groups can be affected by political and economic change. Perhaps the best example of the impact of these changes on interest group is the trade union movement. No other group has suffered so much from the combined effects of political and economic transformation.

THE IMPACT OF POLITICAL AND ECONOMIC CHANGES ON TRADE UNIONS

Many commentators have seen Thatcher as almost the sole cause of the weakness of the trade unions in the 1980s and 1990s. However, as Marsh and King have pointed out, the position of the trade unions was already weakening before she came to power in 1979 and it seems that whatever government had been in power during the 1980s, the trade unions would have had less influence in that decade than they had had in the 1960s and 1970s.[12] In fact, trade unions were affected by a number of economic and social trends:

● **The end of full employment** Full employment placed the trade unions in a very strong position. Whilst there was full employment, trade unions were in a relatively strong bargaining position. With a shortage of labour, the costs of strike action were low and unions could force up the level of wages. Once full employment came to an end in the 1970s, workers were less willing to strike because of the fear of losing their jobs.

● **The decline in large manufacturing industry** This has made it more difficult for trade unions to organise and to strike effectively.

● **The growth of a flexible work force** As manufacturing has declined there has been a shift to a part-time, flexible, increasingly female workforce. This workforce is in a weaker position in terms of taking industrial action and is less likely to be unionised.

● **The decline in union membership** Of unions which are members of the TUC, union density has dropped from 54.5 per cent in 1978 to 40.8 per cent in 1987.[13] In addition, unions such as the Transport and General Workers' Union, AUEW and NUM have seen large drops in membership. Consequently, there has been a large number of amalgamations with the public sector unions forming Unison, the electricians joining the AUEW and the railway unions amalgamating into a single union, the Rail, Maritime and Transport Union.

● **Attitudinal change** In addition to the many other changes, there has been a change in attitude on the part of both employers and employees to trade unions. An increasing number of firms no longer recognise trade unions or will only make single union agreements. Moreover, an increasing number of employees seem happy not to join unions and are prepared to agree salaries on an individual basis.

These social and economic changes have been compounded by the considerable political onslaught to which trade unions have been subjected by Conservative governments. This has comprised hostile action in a number of policy spheres and political arrangements:

● **Economic policy** Conservative economic policy has emphasised defeat of inflation rather than full employment and, whether intentionally or not, has thus weakened the position of trade unions. Conservative governments have been explicit in their desire for a low-wage, deregulated, free-market economy. Reducing the power of the unions has been central to this aim.

● **Incomes policy** In the 1960s and 1970s, industrial relations were made highly political with the introduction of incomes policy. As soon as the Thatcher government was elected, it declared that wages were a matter for unions and employers and that the government would disengage from incomes policy. Consequently, wages have been determined by employers and unions, which has reduced the unions' political influence.

● **The end of corporatism** The Conservative opposition to corporatism caused Thatcher to break off political relations with the trade unions. No longer were they to be involved in detailed economic and social policy discussions in Downing Street. At the same time, many corporatist bodies were either emasculated or abolished.

● **Symbolic confrontations** Conservative governments have been very effective in taking on a number of key trade unions in strikes in order to demonstrate to the trade union movement as a whole that they have the political will to stand up to it. Thatcher was not prepared to be defeated as Heath had been in 1974 and Callaghan was in 1979. Her governments carefully chose a number of strategic battles in which they were prepared to provide the resources necessary to ensure that the unions were defeated. In 1980, the steel union was defeated after a long strike and in 1981 the government outlasted the civil service unions. The most important battle was with the NUM, which was seen as the vanguard of the trade union movement. It was the strongest union in Britain and was well organised and highly politicised. It was also perceived as being responsible for the defeat of the Heath government in 1974. Consequently, the government was determined not to be beaten by the NUM. In 1982 it was willing to meet the NUM's demands because it was not fully prepared for a long strike. By 1984, coal stocks had been built up, necessary legislation was in place, the power workers would clearly not support the miners and a well-integrated police network was in place for dealing with the strike. After a year, the miners returned to work divided and defeated. The 1984-85 miners' strike was crucial in terms of the government's trade union policy. It demonstrated that the government was prepared to take on the most highly-organised British trade union and win. This made it much less likely that other unions would strike.

● **Legislation** The final and most crucial element in the government's industrial relations strategy was a continual stream of legislation that made it increasingly difficult for trade unions to take industrial action. This legislation removed certain trade union immunities, outlawed the closed shop, required ballots for strikes, subjected union leaders to re-election, facilitated selective dismissal of strikers and required ballots for political funds. The combination of legislation made it much more difficult for unions to strike and affected the tactics they could use when striking. During the miners' strike, all NUM funds were frozen because of the union's failure to hold a ballot, and secondary action against storage depots and power stations, which had been so effective in 1974, was illegal.

It is clear that the position of trade unions was greatly affected by the combination of economic change and Thatcherism. However, it is important not to exaggerate the impact of these factors on trade unions. Undoubtedly the position of trade unions has changed but it is important to bear in mind elements of continuity:

● In traditional industries at the shop floor level the organisation of trade union has changed very little.

● Most employers have not made use of trade union legislation.

● The fact that a strike is more difficult to organise now means that strikes often occur as a last resort and with the backing of a ballot. Therefore they have more legitimacy and can be more effective than strikes were in the past.

CONCLUSION

Policy networks were created in a particular economic and ideological context. In the 1980s, pressure groups and policy networks were affected by both economic and political change. Conservative govern-ments had a different idea of the importance and role of pressure groups, which raised a threat to existing policy networks. A further threat was posed by the increasing role of the EU in British politics.

NOTES

1 J Wells, 'Uneven development and de-industrialisation in the UK since 1979' in F Green (ed), *The Restructuring of the UK Economy* (Harvester Wheatsheaf, Hemel Hempstead, 1989).
2 Ibid.
3 P Dunleavy and C Husbands, *British Democracy at the Crossroads* (Allen and Unwin, London, 1985).
4 J Rubery, 'Labour Market Flexibility in Britain' in F Green, op cit.
5 A King, 'Overload: the Problems of Governing in the 1970s', *Political Studies*, 23, 283-96.
6 M Olson, *The Rise and Decline of Nations* (Yale University Press, London, 1982).
7 S Edgell and V Duke, *A Measure of Thatcherism* (HarperCollins, London, 1991).
8 A Gamble, *The Free Economy and Strong State: The Politics of Thatcherism*, second edition (Macmillan, London, 1994).
9 Ibid.
10 *Observer*, 3 July, 1994.
11 A McCulloch and J Moxen, 'Environmental Policy in Scotland: Implementation and the Role of the Voluntary Sector', paper presented to the Political Studies Association Annual Conference, Leicester 20-22 April, 1993.
12 D Marsh and G King 'The Trade Unions under Thatcher', *Essex Papers in Politics and Government*, No.27 (Department of Government, University of Essex, 1986).
13 D Marsh, *The New Politics of British Trade Unionism* (Macmillan, London, 1992).

5 PRESSURE GROUPS AND THE EUROPEAN UNION

Ratification of the Maastricht Treaty in 1993 represented a further stage in the integration of Britain into the European Community, or as it is post-Maastricht, the European Union. An increasing number of decisions, in a wide range of policy areas, is now taken at the European level. This has significant implications for policy making and for pressure groups. For a whole number of policy decisions, the focus for pressure groups is no longer Whitehall but Brussels and this presents pressure groups with new opportunities and threats. In particular, policy networks that have been developed at national level have become, in some cases obsolete, in others significantly less important. Pressure groups have had to become involved in new European networks which frequently present them with a number of difficulties.

POLICY AND POLICY MAKING IN THE EUROPEAN UNION

The two key factors that affect pressure groups with regard to the EU are, first, the increasing policy competence of the EU and, second, the way in which policy is made in the EU.[1]

Originally the role of the Common Market was to act as a free trade customs union which would ensure free trade between member states. However, the founders of the Community always envisaged that it would develop beyond this into a much closer political union. In addition to trade policy, the other key early European policy sector was agriculture. The Common Agricultural Policy (CAP) has for many years been the most comprehensive and expensive European policy. For a long period it was the only policy that was comprehensively determined at Community level. For a while it accounted for at least 75 per cent of the EC budget. This had tremendous implications for domestic agricultural pressure groups.

During the period of British membership of the EU, there has been continual growth in the number of policy areas in which decisions are made at European level. Two events are of particular importance: passage of the Single European Act (SEA) in 1986 and ratification of the Maastricht Treaty in 1993. The SEA committed countries to completing a truly single European market by the end of 1992. In doing so, it laid the foundations for financial and monetary integration. It also widened the base of European policies to include economic and political cohesion, research and technology, the environment and social policy. In order to facilitate policy making in these areas, the Act removed the need for unanimity within the Council of Ministers for policies related to the single market and increased the powers of the European Parliament (EP). As a result the influence of national governments on European policy making was reduced.[2]

The Maastricht Treaty took this process even further. It created a European Union made up of three pillars. The first is the pre-existing European Community which is responsible for economic and social issues. The second is internal security policy concerned with policy matters such as drugs, terrorism and immigration. This is an intergovernmental pillar and therefore the Commission does not have power over decisions and unanimity still applies. The third is foreign and security policy which is also intergovernmental.

Maastricht extended qualified majority voting (QMV)[3] to a new range of policy areas, including the free movement of capital, transport, social policy, research and technology and the environment. The power of the EP was also increased so that it has a right to a second reading of legislation passed through QMV and can block certain measures.

These changes have major implications for pressure groups. They mean that a number of issues that were previously decided at national level are now decided in Europe. If groups are to have any influence they have to lobby at the European level. Moreover, with the introduction of QMV, national governments can no longer veto a range of policies. In the past, pressure groups could rely on national governments to protect certain interests. Now they are much more dependent on winning support at the EU level. Furthermore, the way in which policy is made in Brussels is more complicated than in Britain and this has important implications for pressure-group tactics and policy networks.

In Britain, the system of government is remarkably centralised. Power is almost completely concentrated in the executive. Regional government does not exist, local government is weak, and the executive dominates parliament. This, in a sense, makes life easy for pressure groups. They know where to target their resources. In another sense it makes life difficult. If groups fail to gain access to the executive they are unlikely to have much influence. The EU, by contrast, has a very fragmented and diverse policy-making system with many different decision-making centres and a wide range of access points. It is easier for interest groups to gain access to European decision making, but more difficult for them to influence policy because so many institutions and compromises are involved in making policy.

The key institutions within the EU are the Commission, the Council of Ministers, and the EP. The role of the Commission is to initiate policy. In doing so, it negotiates widely with interest groups and governments. Often the process of policy initiation is one of complex bargaining with the Commission attempting to achieve a compromise between a range of sectional and national interests.

The Commission is made up of a range of Directorates General (DGs) that have specific responsibilities. DG VI is concerned with agriculture, DG XI with the environment. Each Directorate has a range of formal and informal contacts with pressure groups. DG VI is in almost daily contact with the Committee of Professional Agricultural Organisations (COPA), the European farmers' group. There are also continuous and close informal contacts between farmers and Commission officials.

Formal consultation between groups and the Commission takes place through the EU's Economic and Social Committee (ESC) and the advisory committees of each Directorate General. The ESC comprises 189 representatives of employers, workers and other groups. All Commission proposals go to the ESC for comment but it rarely has much influence on decisions. Advisory committees exist in each DG and are made up of groups directly concerned with the respective policy area. The concern of advisory committees is to advise the Commission on implementation of its directives.

The most powerful body in the EU is the Council of Ministers. It is the Council of Ministers that has the power to accept or reject policy. According to Mazey and Richardson:

> The fact that there is a considerable concentration of power within the Council, that its meetings are secret and closed, and that groups have no direct access to it, has significant implications for EC lobbying styles.[4]

Groups have little option but to lobby through their national ministries and are dependent on national ministers and officials to protect their interests.

A consequence of the position of the Council is that British officials in Brussels are both lobbyists and targets for lobbyists. Officials lobby both for national interest groups and for domestic government departments. A large part of their role is to ensure that national interests are not infringed. However, they also have to ensure that interest groups and government departments know the limits of negotiation. They have to make domestic interests aware of how far they can go.[5]

The SEA and the Maastricht Treaty have also made the EP more influential. It now has the right to a second reading of much legislation and some strong powers in relation to the EU budget. It is therefore increasingly a target for pressure group activities. 'In the period between the introduction of the Single European Act in 1987 and November 1990, the Commission accepted 1,052 of the parliaments 1724 amendments to single market laws, and of those the Council agreed to 719.'[6] Consequently, the EP now provides a forum for pressure groups to achieve changes to the detail of legislation.

The policy-making process in Brussels is extremely complex involving a range of DGs, Councils of Ministers and national governments. A continual process of negotiation between national and commission officials, the EP and a myriad of interests groups takes place. Pressure groups have a range of strategies that they can adopt. They can go through governments or through Euro-groups to the Commission, through the EP and through a series of formal advisory committees.

This complexity has important implications for pressure groups and the EU. What is interesting and difficult about EU policy making is that the EU is an international organisation that shares many features of a domestic state: it is concerned with ameliorating internal pressures in order to make domestic rather than foreign policy. Yet it is very different from a state, particularly the British state, in that it has a number of decision making centres and a high number of access points. It lacks a monopoly of authoritative control of a territorial area and is thus in a position of having to reconcile conflicting national interests. It also lacks the ability to implement policy and therefore has limited control over the implementation process.

These factors make policy networks important within the EU and useful for understanding the way policy is made. In a system of multiple decision-making centres and a range of conflicting interests policy networks are a way of organising the policy process. They help to:

● **Generate consensus** The range of conflicting interests is much greater in Brussels than in Britain. In Whitehall many groups are excluded. At the European level exclusion is more difficult as any given policy area will involve more groups. The range of interests also has to be multiplied by the nations involved and this adds a national dimension to sectional interests. In agricultural policy, for example, there are often major conflicts between southern Mediterranean countries concerned with vegetable, olive oil and wine production and Northern countries concerned with cereal and livestock production.

● **Make sense of the policy process** Policy networks as a mechanism of inclusion and exclusion are even more important at the European level than at the domestic. They enable policy makers to make some sense of the policy process and of the conflicting interests within it.

● **Produce coordination between various groups and institutions at the European level** Because so many interests and institutions are involved in policy making, development of policy networks is a way of coordinating the various actors and of building coalitions. Policy networks provide a mechanism through which the different actors can contact each other.

● **Ensure service delivery** Policy networks which link European policy making to service delivery are crucial for policy implementation. The EU has a very small bureaucracy. It is only a policy-making organisation and relies on national governments for implementation. Consequently, pressure groups are very important in terms of providing information both on policy and on policy implementation. It is important for the Commission to develop the types of networks which enable it to develop informational links with pressure groups.

The paradox of European policy making is that whilst policy networks are important in terms of managing both relations with pressure groups and the policy process, the nature of the European policy process makes policy networks difficult to develop and sustain.

The features of the EU which make policy networks important – openness, conflicts of interest, the role of nation states in policy making – also undermine policy networks. The range of interests involved in policy making, the fact that there are often conflicts of national interest in policy-making and the fact that nation states can on occasion override or ignore EU policy means that policy networks are very unstable. Issues which at the domestic level would be highly technical and depoliticised can easily become politicised if national interests are seen to be involved. When Thatcher was British prime minister, agricultural policy, which involves one of the most closed networks in Europe, frequently became politicised because issues of agricultural reform were linked to Britain's budgetary contribution.

Although policy networks do exist at the European level, they thus tend to be more open and more unstable than those which are found in Britain. The number of groups, decision-making centres and conflicts of ideology and interest means that they are more likely to be at the issue network than the policy community end of the continuum. Even when they are relatively closed, they can quickly become politicised when issues of national interest are involved. The complexity of European policy making means that pressure groups often act differently in Europe than they do in Britain.

PRESSURE GROUP ACTIVITY IN THE EUROPEAN UNION

The complexities of the EU decision-making process require pressure groups to organise and act differently at the European level. There are two distinctive features of European lobbying. First, the nature of the EU as both an intergovernmental organisation and a policy-making institution means that different types of interest are involved. Second, the nature of the EU prompts a whole range of different strategies for influencing EU policy.

Policy making at the European level introduces a number of interests into policy networks. These include:

● **Domestic pressure groups** Pressure groups that operate in Britain, or any other EU (or even non-EU) country, can lobby the institutions of the EU. Many pressure groups that operate in Britain realise the importance of the European level and focus much of their activity on it. It is now commonplace for British pressure groups to have offices in Brussels and to employ lobbying consultants to work for them at the European level. Obviously, the first groups represented in Brussels were those initially affected by EC policy, in particular farmers and industrial interests. However, it is increasingly important for groups involved with the environment, consumer affairs, social policy, immigration and many other policy areas to have access to the European level of policy making. This, of course, has advantages and disadvantages for groups that might be outsiders in Britain. It has advantages in that the European level is much more open. Where they fail to achieve access at the national level, they may have a second chance at the European. Whilst British trade unions and local authorities have been excluded from policy making in Britain, they have found the EU relatively receptive to their lobbying. The disadvantage is that money and expertise are required to operate at the European level. It is very difficult for poorly-resourced domestic consumer and environmental groups to compete with producer groups in Europe. To mount a continual lobbying campaign in Brussels requires finance to maintain staff abroad and knowledge of the European policy process. Consequently, groups are increasingly seeking to exercise influence through Eurogroups.

● **The formation of Eurogroups** One way for British groups to attempt to influence EU policy making is through joining European federations of groups. It is only Eurogroups that can be represented on the ESC and the Commission's advisory committees. In principle, though not in practice, only Eurogroups can have contact with the Commission. By 1990, it was estimated that there were more than 500 Eurogroups with over-representation in the areas of agriculture and the food industry.[7] There are now Eurogroups in a range of areas. Examples are the European Environmental Bureau and the Bureau Européen de Consommateurs. Eurogroups have three main functions. They enable different interests within the EU to keep abreast of policy developments and to have early warning of policy initiatives. They provide an organisation to lobby the various institutions of the Union. They allow national associations to keep in touch with their European counterparts and, when necessary, lobby each other. McLaughlin and Jordan[8] indicate that very close networks can be established between the Commission and Eurogroups. DGs tend to be concerned with the regulation of activity in one sector and therefore need to be aware of the interests of the key groups in that sector. Moreover, they often need the information and support of the Eurogroups in order to develop policy initiatives. Groups that have developed close relationships with DGs are in a strong position to become involved at a very early stage of the policy process. However, at least some Eurogroups have major weaknesses. Frequently, they are unable to develop a consensus between the various national and sectoral interests which they represent. In 1990, the Committee of Common Market Automobile Constructors collapsed due to its inability to develop a consensus on key aspects of policy.[9]

● **National governments** National governments frequently lobby for national interests within European institutions. However, it is important to realise that national ministers and civil servants do not only lobby for national interests. They also defend sectional interests. Within the Council of Ministers, departmental ministers negotiate with their foreign counterparts and are aware of the preferences of their domestic interests in the lobbying process. British agricultural ministers have long defended headage subsidies for British sheep farmers which other agricultural ministers have wanted to abolish. British civil servants frequently fly to Brussels to discuss and negotiate policy. Again they are aware of the demands of the interests within their domestic policy networks and attempt to ensure that their interests are defended at the European level.

● **Non-EU countries and groups** A number of nations and non-EU groups are aware of the impact that EU policy can have on their interests and therefore are involved in lobbying in Europe and establishing European offices. The EU committee of the American Chambers of Commerce has 'possibly the most effective lobbying organization in Brussels and has developed a complex and expert structure of specialist committees which represent an unrivalled network of advance intelligence within the EC'.[10]

● **Regional and local government** Local government in the UK and regional government in much of the rest of the EU is becoming increasingly aware of the impact of Europe on sub-national units. As British local authorities have found central government increasingly impervious to their demands they have extended their lobbying efforts in Europe. Many cities have been successful in gaining development grants from the EU. The Coalfields Community Campaign has brought together local authorities in regions affected by coal mine closures concerned to persuade the Commission to create a new development fund. Creation of the RECHAR programme is the result of this lobbying effort. British local authorities have become part of transnational networks involving different European regions and a range of sectional interest groups focused on the EU. Local authorities are involved in networks concerned with areas affected by automobiles, textiles, seaside towns, social issues and much else besides.[11]

The EU policy process has more access points than do its national counterparts. More strategies are therefore open to pressure groups:

● **National strategy** The easiest route for pressure groups is to lobby at the national level in order to persuade government to protect their interests in Europe. If government or a minister sees the sectional interest of a group as being in the national interest, that group is in a very strong position. National government may defend its interests within the Council of Ministers. One reason why the British government opted out of the Social Charter was because British employers, the CBI, the Institute of Directors and individual large companies argued that it would raise labour costs, reduce profitability and increase unemployment. Consequently, the British government argued this case in negotiations over the Maastricht Treaty.

● **Brussels and the Commission** With the introduction of QMV in a wide range of policy areas, interest groups can no longer rely on national governments to protect their interests. It is therefore much more important that they develop contacts with the Commission. The Brussels bureaucracy is much more open than its Whitehall counterpart and the aim of interest groups is to develop informal and formal contacts with Commission officials so that they can be involved in early stages of policy development.

● **The European Parliament** The Maastricht Treaty also increased the power of the EP and made it an increasingly important target for pressure. The EP is often receptive to interests that are excluded by national governments and the Commission, such as consumers and environmentalists.

● **The European Court of Justice** The ECJ is responsible for interpretation and implementation of European law. An increasing number of interest groups use it to ensure that governments implement EU legislation. Environmental groups have used the ECJ to force governments to implement legislation on cleaning water supplies.[11] In another case, an ECJ decision has forced the British Ministry of Defence to pay large amounts of compensation to women in the armed forces who were sacked when they became pregnant.

POLICY NETWORKS AND THE EUROPEAN UNION

Britain's EU membership greatly affects the way in which policy is made and the activities and strategies of pressure groups. It also has important implications for policy networks. Many policy networks, rather than organising at a domestic level, now organise at the European level. This often changes the nature of policy networks. A new variety of interest groups is involved. Instead of one decision-making centre, there may be three or four with the Council of Ministers, the Commission, national governments and the EP. This increases the likelihood of conflict within a network because of the number of national and sectional interests involved in a particular policy area. As a result, European policy making is more likely to be characterised by issue networks than by policy communities. Nevertheless, two examples from the environmental and agricultural policy spheres demonstrate that both types of network exist.

In the environmental sphere, Bomberg shows that the policy arena is characterised by a high level of conflict between a large number of actors and much policy change. The network is highly permeable to many interests and is frequently highly political. Moreover, there is a large number of actors, including DG XI, other DGs, national civil servants, scientists, the EP, environmental pressure groups and business groups. In addition, the network is frequently subject to a high level of media attention. At various points in the policy process it is possible that national civil servants, experts on Council working groups and Commission committees enter and exit the network. Who is actually involved at any particular time depends on the issue.

Bomberg cites the case of waste packaging in which 16 different DGs were involved in policy development. In addition, more than 50 Euro-groups, a number of non-governmental organisations and a range of trade and industry groups took part in policy discussions. The EP also played a role in development of legislation and in doing so further increased the range of actors involved in the issue. The result of divisions and conflict within the network was a weaker directive on waste packaging than either the Commission or the EP wanted.[13]

In contrast to environmental policy, agricultural policy has always been made within a relatively closed policy community. Although the number of actors involved in agricultural policy increased when Britain and other states joined the EC in the 1970s and 1980s, this did not have much impact on the way in which agricultural policy is made. European agricultural policy involves the Commission through DG VI, the Council of Agricultural Ministers and a range of agricultural interest groups. Nevertheless, the policy process remains relatively closed. The belief of those involved in agricultural policy making is that the CAP should aim to increase both agricultural production and farm incomes. This is a consensus amongst those in the policy community. Groups which question this consensus on grounds of consumer or environmental costs are considered to have broken the rules of the game and are excluded from policy making. In addition, decision-making organisations involved in agricultural policy, such as national agricultural ministries and DG VI of the Commission, have very close relations with farmers' groups and tend to exclude consumer or environmental groups. Consumers, environmentalists and the DGs concerned with these issues have very little impact on European agricultural policy. The Council of Agricultural Ministers is the final decision-making body in agricultural policy and is made up of national agricultural ministers each of whom has very close relationships with national farm groups. As a consequence, despite the very high cost of the CAP and the fact that it produces food that has to be destroyed or dumped, the policy has been very difficult to reform. Even in the 1990s, after years of domestic and international pressure for reform, the policy community has managed to ensure that it retains control of agricultural policy making and that a high proportion of EU funds is still spent on agriculture. In recent years, the high level of criticism that the CAP has attracted has certainly changed the agricultural policy community. Reforms have meant that farmers receive lower prices than was the case in the past and environmental concerns have received increased attention. Nevertheless, farmers are still in a privileged position and in Britain they now receive large sums of money for not growing food in order to avoid the political embarrassment of over-production.

CONCLUSION

Britain's membership of the EU has had important implications for pressure groups. On a whole range of issues attention now has to be directed at Brussels rather than Whitehall. This has certain advantages in that the European bureaucracy is more open to pressure groups than is the British. Nevertheless, the number of interests and decision-making centres involved also makes it more difficult for pressure groups to establish the close relationships which allow them really to influence policy. The range of groups involved, combined with the prevalence of and sectional and national conflicts, makes the development of closed-policy communities very difficult. Consequently, the EU has started to undermine some of the policy networks established at the domestic level.

NOTES

1 For a general overview of politics and policy in the EC up to the creation of the EU at the end of 1993, see A Geddes, *Britain in the European Community* (Baseline Books, Manchester, 1993).

2 S Mazey and J J Richardson, (eds), *Lobbying in the European Community* (Oxford University Press, Oxford, 1993).

3 Qualified majority voting (QMV) means that the Council of Ministers can make policy through majority voting. However, national votes are weighted according to a nations' size and three nations can form a 'blocking minority'. See S Ludlam, 'Parliamentary or Executive Sovereignty', *Politics Review*, Vol.3, No.4. p.28.

4 Mazey and Richardson, op cit, p.14.

5 D Spence, 'The Role of the National Civil Service in European Lobbying: The British Case', in Mazey and Richardson, op cit.

6 Mazey and Richardson, op cit., p.11.

7 A Butt Philip, 'British Pressure Groups and the European Community' in S George, *Britain and the European Community* (Clarendon Press, Oxford, 1992).

8 A McLaughlin and G Jordan, 'The Rationality of Lobbying in Europe: Why are Euro-Groups so Numerous and so Weak?', in Mazey and Richardson, op. cit.

9 Ibid.

10 Mazey and Richardson, op cit., p.7.

11 J Bennington and J Harvey, 'Spheres or Tiers? The Significance of Transnational Local Authority Networks', in P Dunleavy and J Stanyer, *Contemporary Political Studies*, 1994, Vol 2. (PSA, Belfast, 1994).

12 Mazey and Richardson, op cit.

13 E. Bomberg, 'Issue Networks and the Environment: Explaining EU Environmental Policy', paper presented at the Political Studies Annual Conference, Swansea, 29-31 March 1994.

6 POLICY NETWORKS AND NEW SOCIAL MOVEMENTS

Policy networks have tended to be dominated by particular types of group. Groups with access to the policy process are those which control key economic resources. Policy networks have thus been dominated largely by economic groups, such as trade unions or business groups, or by professional groups, such as doctors. However, it is increasingly argued that economic, social and political change has led to the rise of NSMs and that these movements challenge both the traditional political agenda and established policy networks. They introduce new issues and new interests into the political process. This chapter examines NSMs, and assesses why they have emerged and the impact they have had on the policy process.

DEFINING NEW SOCIAL MOVEMENTS

Traditionally it is argued that pressure groups are concerned with 'productionist' issues. They are on the whole linked to producer interests, whether they be those of doctors or teachers producing services or workers producing cars, coal or whatever. These groups tend to be interested in a specific set of economic issues that are related directly to the interests of their members. They use their position in the production of goods as an economic lever to influence government policy. Consequently, they have the resources necessary to obtain a place within a policy community.

The politics of NSMs is concerned with challenging the established political order with its emphasis on productionist issues and its tendency to make decisions in closed policy arenas which prevent most of the public from having any say in the decision-making process. The 'New Politics' focuses on issues such as the environment, pollution, peace, minority rights, and participation. NSMs tend to use alternative tactics, such as demonstrations and boycotts, rather than consultation and are predominantly supported by the educated middle class.[1] The main characteristics of NSMs are as follows:

● **They are primarily social** Often the concerns of NSMs are not 'political' but cultural. They aim to empower individuals within the social sphere rather than gain political power as such.

● **They are located within civil society** The focus of much NSM activity is not the state but society. They are concerned with how people live together, the nature of social conflict and alternative ways in which society can be organised. Often they attempt to keep the state out of their areas of interest.[2]

● **They attempt to develop and use new forms of knowledge** Old politics is generally organised around the notion that there is some objective truth that, if discovered, can provide the necessary information to develop the right public policy to solve a particular problem. NSMs challenge this traditional conception of knowledge and develop their own sources of information and exchanges of knowledge.

● **They develop alternative types of organisation** NSMs are concerned with democracy, participation, decentralisation, community and small organisation. They are dedicated to ending the domination of industrial society by hierarchical, elitist organisations. They want to develop forms of politics that are based on participation within the community. Large organisations mean that individuals become lost, have no control over their own lives and are subject to government by arbitrary rules. If decisions are made within the community, all members can participate and the rules that govern the society can be related to the concerns of the people they affect. The goal of many NSMs is to achieve a non-hierarchical participatory society. They therefore organise their interest groups on this basis. Consequently, they frequently do not have clearly identified leaders, they organise on a local basis and much of their political activity is focused on 'consciousness raising' rather than on implementing policies prescribed by political leaders.

● **They tactics are based on direct action** Because NSMs do not have access to policy networks they can seldom influence policy through consultation with civil servants and ministers. In addition, some NSMs see themselves as ideological outsiders and therefore believe that contact with the political system will result in dilution of their goals. For these reasons, NSMs tend to rely on direct action. Most often this takes the form of marches and demonstrations. Some groups are prepared to undertake illegal action. Greenpeace, for example, defied a court order to block the waste pipe from Sellafield nuclear reprocessing plant.

● **They have a distinctive ideology** Most NSMs are concerned to challenge the existing balance of power and wealth in society. They have an ideology that is critical of the existing political and social structure. They are interested in issues relating to the quality of life and therefore emphasise issues of democracy and the environment above the traditional concerns of economic growth. Consequently, most NSMs see themselves as ideological outsiders and are not prepared to compromise with the existing political system.

● **Their membership is not class-based** Most NSMs are non-class groups. They tend to promote issues, such as peace, the environment and civil rights, that cut across a range of class issues. However, there is a strong tendency for the middle class to be over-represented in NSM membership. Nevertheless, they do not become members in order to promote middle-class interests but to promote specific issues.

● **They provide a radical alternative to Marxism** For most of the twentieth century the radical critique of existing social organisation has been based on Marxism. It sees the working class as a potentially revolutionary actor that has the economic resources to overthrow the existing political system and replace it with a new model of social organisation. Most NSMs reject the central tenets of Marxism. They do not believe that there is a single revolutionary class and a single model of transformation, or that the creation of a socialist state will necessarily ensure desirable alternatives. NSMs propose a radicalism that is not based purely on economic issues or on class but on community, individual rights and participation. Hence, for NSMs the focus of political activity is often not the state but society.

● **They do not promote one particular way of organising society** They believe that it is important to build alliances between groups supporting different issues and between old and new social movements. Unlike Marxists, NSMs do not see right and wrong answers and right and wrong political movements.

NSMs are radical groups that question the existing political and social order. Their concerns are wider than sectional interests. They either focus on the rights of broad social groups, such as women, gays or ethnic minorities, or they focus on issues, such as the environment or peace. They tend to be organised along non-hierarchical lines and to be concerned with issues of rights, democracy and participation. Nevertheless, it has to be remembered that there is a broad variety of NSMs. Some – for example, particular environmental groups – tend to take very traditional organisational forms and are prepared to engage in established politics. Others – for example, New Age travellers – want completely to disengage from the political system and are concerned to establish their own sphere of social organisation outside the traditional structures of society.

NSMs seem to have developed particularly in the 1960s as part of the process that generated student riots in Europe and the United States. Within these protest movements can be seen elements of the environmental, women's, civil rights and peace movements. This raises the question why it was that these new groups entered the political stage in the 1960s and 1970s.

THE GROWTH OF NEW SOCIAL MOVEMENTS

A wide range of factors has been advanced to explain the growth of NSMs. They include:

● **The rise of post-industrial society** Britain has been substantially affected by economic change. It is argued by some theorists of NSMs that changes such as the decline of manufacturing, the rise of the service sector and the growth of the information society have transformed industrial societies into post-industrial ones. For Bell, power is not related to economic resources but derives from control of information. Therefore, groups become more concerned with knowledge and information rather than with economic issues.

● **The rise of post-material values** Inglehart argues that post-industrial society has ensured that a large number of people are no longer economically insecure. As a result, people's priorities have shifted from materialist values (concerns about economic and physical security) to post-material values (issues of self-expression and the quality of life). He further argues that there has been a generational shift. Those born before 1945 are primarily materialist. Those born after are evenly split between materialism and post-materialism. Post-materialists are most likely to be members of NSMs. European countries with most post-materialists will have greater numbers of NSMs.

● **The decline of the working class and the labour movement** For André Gorz, changes in the pattern of production, notably the growth of a flexible workforce and the decline of large manufacturing units, mean that worker power is no longer a possible method of transforming the social and political structure. Workers are now in a minority and most people do not identify with the working class. Consequently, the labour movement is no longer an agent of social change. As a result, NSMs have risen as alternative organisations for achieving social change.

● **Disillusionment with traditional politics** Poll evidence suggests that people are becoming disillusioned with traditional political parties. The persistence of unemployment and of rising levels of crime, combined with the growth of an underclass, indicate to some people that such parties are no longer able to solve economic and social problems. In consequence, people are either withdrawing from politics, as is demonstrated by the decline in party membership and voting turnouts, or turning to alternative types of politics. In response to government road-building policies, there have, for instance, been increasing numbers of demonstrations, which have built alliances between radical green groups and traditional middle-class homeowners. Such people now have little faith in traditional political channels responding to their interests. They are, therefore, turning increasingly to direct action.

Increased wealth, changing patterns of production and disillusionment with traditional modes of politics seem to have given rise to NSMs. However, it is important not to exaggerate the situation. Recent elections in Britain seem to suggest that economic issues are still paramount in voters' minds when it comes to choosing a government. In the 1992 British general election, a key factor in the victory of the Conservative party was fear of Labour's tax plans and a belief that the Conservatives could be better trusted with economic management. Most people are not members of NSMs and are still prepared to limit their political activity to the traditional activity of voting. However, there has undoubtedly been a rise in NSMs and they are having an increasing impact on the policy process.

THE IMPACT OF NEW SOCIAL MOVEMENTS

It is impossible to establish the size of NSM memberships. Frequently, NSMs do not have formal membership lists. They involve people in political activity without obliging them consciously to join an organisation. Frequently, they are made up of autonomous local groups which have little or no central organisation. The women's movement is made up of a range of different and unconnected organisations, such as women involved in local self-help groups, and women who become involved through engaging in feminist ideas. It is estimated that about 3.5 million people are members of environmental groups whilst many more promote environmental goals. CND had a large membership in the 1980s and it is clear that the women's movement has involved millions of women in a range of different groups and forms of activities.

Wainwright has argued that NSMs have begun to challenge the monopoly of social change held by parties of the left in western Europe. They now rival both social democratic and communist parties in developing a new political agenda which is concerned with social as well as economic issues and in providing alternative forums for radical people to participate in political activity. As party membership has declined, membership of NSMs has increased.

Wainwright further argues that the impact of NSMs can be seen in the ending of the Cold War. She argues that the peace movement might not have been successful in preventing the siting of cruise missiles in Europe, but that it did create pressure throughout society for the development of *perestroika*. The peace movement shifted political debate away from the constraints of simple Cold War antagonisms. It also kept the issue continually in the news. Through grassroots activities, such as the Greenham Common peace camp and attempts to track the movements of cruise missiles, the peace movement maintained a high profile for the issues of nuclear proliferation.

The peace movement thus contributed to the end of the Cold War but not in precisely the way that its activists intended. They eased the way for *perestroika* and the peaceful collapse of communism. They damaged the Cold War consensus, or ensured that it could not be remade. But they did not fatally wound the institutions of the Cold War, as most activists had hoped.[3]

The impact of NSMs on traditional policy networks can be best highlighted if we examine two case studies: the women's and the environmental movements. Both have been highly successful in shifting the political agenda and in provoking detailed policy change. They have also been diverse movements involving a vast array of groups, activities and goals.

THE WOMEN'S MOVEMENT

Some sort of women's movement, concerned with issues such as women's legal rights, maternity issues, contraception and, perhaps most famously, the suffragette campaign to gain the right to vote for women, has existed in Britain since the late nineteenth century, if not before. The broad-based women's movement that we know today was really started in the 1960s.

In the 1950s and 1960s, there were increasing educational and employment opportunities for women. Expansion of the university sector meant that greater numbers of women went into higher education. Full employment created a demand for women to leave the home and join the labour market. At the same time, an increasing amount of American literature questioned the traditional role of women and argued that women were not happy as housewives.

In the late 1960s, the changing economic and educational position of women and the increased questioning of their traditional position was affected by the radical students' movement. This movement was frequently concerned with issues of equality and civil rights but it paid relatively little attention to the role of women. Many women involved in the students' movement therefore began to form their own groups and organisations and started to campaign for the rights of women. This led to the establishment of the equal rights association.

The first important issue that really established the women's movement was the equal pay struggle. In 1968, women workers at Ford went on strike to demand equal pay with men. This issue was not supported by the union but gained the support of elements of the women's movement outside the factory. For the first time, the more middle-class, radical feminist movement joined with working-class women to promote a practical and easily identifiable issue. The strike was given a great deal of publicity and eventually obliged Barbara Castle, Minister for Employment, to support an equal pay bill.

In the 1970s, the British feminist movement began rapidly to grow. It was split into a number of different strands and tactics. Liberal feminists tended to work through traditional political organisations, such as parties and unions, and through traditional political mechanisms, in order to campaign on particular issues. Radical and socialist feminists believed that changes in the position of women could only be achieved through changes in the political and social system. They were either connected to radical left groups or formed their own small consciousness-raising groups.

However, in Oxford in 1970, attempts were made to organise and unite the various strands of feminism. A Women's National Co-ordinating Committee was set up to provide information to various groups and to co-ordinate campaigns. It was agreed that the women's movement should operate outside the conventional political system.

Four aims were laid down: equal pay; equal opportunities in education; free contraception and abortion; and free 24-hour child care.

This initiative was not very successful at uniting the various strands within the women's movement. There was a tendency towards factionalism and division. However, the mid-1970s did see some major gains in terms of women's rights. The Labour government passed the Equal Pay Act and the Sexual Discrimination Act. Formally, the women's movement achieved three of its four Oxford aims. However, this exacerbated tensions within the movement. Many feminists saw the Acts as being full of loopholes and an attempt to co-opt the movement. Certain sections became more radical and separatist whilst others became part of a women's policy network, working with, and in, institutions, such as the Equal Opportunities Commission. For those women who were prepared to work within the system, the key issues became enforcement of equal rights and pay. Legal measures were important mechanisms in extending their rights.

However, the late 1970s and the 1980s saw, to some extent, reversals for the women's movement. The position of women in society was affected by two factors. One was economic recession. The other was the rise of New Right ideology. Economic recession affected women in a number of ways. It meant that many of their demands, such as greater job opportunities and increased child care, were marginalised. In addition, women were disproportionately affected by recession. An increasing feminisation of poverty pushed women into low-paid jobs or forced them to bring up families on social security. Unions and political parties became less concerned with the demands of women and more concerned with directly materialist issues, such as jobs and economic growth. New Right ideology also had a detrimental impact on the women's movement. The Thatcher governments believed that women should be in the home and that government did not have a positive duty to protect the rights of women. Equality has not been a central concern of Conservative governments in the 1980s and 1990s. To a large extent, women's issues have been ignored as governments have been more concerned with cutting labour costs and the amount of money spent on social security.

Nevertheless, the impact of the women's movement has been demonstrated by changes in the political agenda. There is undoubtedly much greater awareness of the rights of women in the 1990s than in the 1950s and 1960s. Even the Conservative chancellor, Nigel

Lawson, abolished some of the worst gender anomalies in the taxation system. The women's movement has largely managed to protect abortion legislation passed in the 1960s, despite several attempts to make it more restrictive. After the 1992 general election, John Major appeared to respond to criticism that there were no women in his cabinet by promoting Virginia Bottomley to health secretary and Gillian Shepherd to agriculture secretary. He also initiated 'Opportunity 2000' with the explicit aim of increasing the number of women in senior positions in business and the civil service. The Labour Party has also shifted quite a long way on women. It is now compulsory for every Labour shortlist for a parliamentary seat to include at least one woman and Labour is committed dramatically to increase the number of women MPs. Tony Blair's first shadow cabinet contained five women. Labour also proposes a ministry of women.

Perhaps most important for the women's movement are not changes in the political sphere but changes in civil society. Despite continued inequality in senior management, there are now many more women employed in traditional male areas than in the past. Certain occupations, such medicine and law, have almost equal numbers of men and women. Indeed, women are becoming a very large part of the labour force. Despite the problems, fragmentation and set-backs of the women's movement, it has shifted the political debate and succeeded in changing perceptions of women.[4]

THE ENVIRONMENTAL MOVEMENT

The environmental movement is probably the best supported in Britain. Like the women's movement it has a long history. Many environmental groups have existed since the nineteenth century. However, as with feminism, it was only in the 1960s that what we know today as environmentalism really developed. An explosion of environmental groups took place partly as a result of the students' movement and also because of a more general awareness of the impact of urbanisation and modern technology on the environment. Increased living standards were placing greater demands on the environment.

In common with the women's movement, the environmental movement has split into insiders ('light greens') and outsiders ('dark greens'). Insiders, such as the National Trust and the RSPB, have attempted to work within the system for piecemeal legislation. They believe that the environment can be protected through regulation. Outsiders believe that the environment can only be protected if fundamental changes are made to the nature of the industrial system and the way we live. For them, the very nature of society has to be changed. It must be made sustainable, ending – or greatly reducing – the use of fossil fuels and eliminating the wasteful use of consumer goods. To save the environment, we must change how we live.

Certain environmental groups, including one of the largest, FoE, have moved from being outsiders to being partial insiders. Government has become increasingly aware of environmental issues and has been prepared to consult closely with FoE over issues of pollution control, carbon dioxide emissions, pesticides in water and global warming.

The environmental movement has been successful in placing environmental issues on the political agenda. It has also achieved some significant victories. It has forced government to promote lead reduction in petrol; it has persuaded it to modify its road-building plan and to make a commitment to reducing carbon dioxide levels. It has forced water companies to improve water quality.

Perhaps the greatest success of the environmental movement came at the EP elections of 1989 when it appeared that the Green Party had gained widespread popular support with 15 per cent of the vote. The immediate impact was to force the government and opposition parties to shift towards a more environmental position. The government produced a White Paper, *Our Common Inheritance*, which outlined environmental taxes and increased environmental regulation.

However, it appears that the Greens benefitted partly from protest votes and partly from increased environmental concern at a time of economic boom. With the onset of recession in the 1990s, popular concern with the environment seems to have lessened. Government commitments in the White Paper have been forgotten and support for the Green Party has almost disappeared, though this is partly the result of internal splits.

Despite this setback, environmental issues are still on the political agenda. Political parties have to pay lip service to the environment. In addition, the EU is becoming increasingly important in terms of environmental policy. Often the higher environmental standards of continental countries are being imposed on Britain. The formal position of the Union is that the environmental impact of all policies should be considered at the policy-making stage. Environmental groups have been very successful in using the ECJ to ensure that Britain adopts European environmental regulations.

The impact of environmental groups has not been solely in the political arena but also in the social sphere of civil society. Increasing numbers of people are aware of environmental issues. Many people recycle waste, use unleaded petrol and buy ozone-friendly fridges. There are increasing demands on supermarkets to provide environmentally-friendly products. The environment may have become a marketing tool but it demonstrates a high degree of awareness of environmental issues and an attempt by people to change their lifestyles.[5]

Both the women's and the environmental movements provide good examples of the key features of NSMs. They are both movements rather than groups in that they contain a wide array of political organisations and actors, a range of tactics and many goals. They often focus their activity on how people live rather than on the political system and they are concerned with issues that are not directly material. Both developed in periods of economic growth and have succeeded chiefly in periods of affluence. Both are largely middle-class movements but have made inroads into the working class. Both have had limited success in changing policy but greater success in changing attitudes and issues on the political agenda.

NEW SOCIAL MOVEMENTS AND POLICY NETWORKS

To a large extent, NSMs have been excluded from policy networks because they challenge the interests of traditionally powerful groups. However, they have had an impact on policy networks. The environmental movement has had limited access to a range of networks, such as transport, agriculture and water, and has even made some important political gains. However, the greatest impact of these social movements on policy networks is in challenging the political agenda. They have forced networks to consider new issues and, in doing so, have had some success in opening networks to new ideas and new groups. They may not have had a significant impact on policy but they have been successful in limiting the activity of networks and ensuring that issues raised by NSMs are considered.

NOTES

1 D Jahn, *New Politics in Trade Unions* (Dartmouth, Aldershot, 1993).
2 A Scott, *Ideology and New Social Movements* (Unwin Hyman, London, 1990).
3 H Wainwright, *Arguments for a New Left* (Blackwell, Oxford, 1993).
4 The section on the women's movement is based on E Wilson, *Only Halfway to Paradise: Women in Post-War Britain* (Tavistock, London, 1980).
5 For more details, see S Young, *The Politics of the Environment* (Baseline Books, Manchester, 1993).

7 THE CHANGING FOOD POLICY COMMUNITY

The food policy community is an interesting example of pressure group politics. It contains a range of powerful interests, yet it has still been subject to considerable change. For most of the post-war period, the relationship between food and health was not political. Once the problem of rationing was ended in the early 1950s and Britons were ensured a secure supply of food, food was no longer subject to political debate. The government's role in food policy was to ensure that food of a reasonable quality was supplied at a fair price. This was managed largely through agricultural policy, a limited nutritional policy to ensure minimum standards[1] and legislation on storage and handling of food to guarantee safety. Most of these issues were seen as technical and were not subject to widespread political debate. Food was not a political issue. The 1980s, however, saw food become highly political. A wide range of issues – heart disease, pesticides in food, salmonella, nutrition and Bovine Spongiform Encephalopathy (BSE) – burst on to the political agenda. The questions that arise are why did food – which is so central to our lives – remain apolitical for so long? And why did it quite suddenly become political in the 1980s? Answers to these questions may be found in the nature of the food policy community and changes that affected it in the 1980s.

THE FOOD POLICY COMMUNITY

During World War Two food was a highly political issue. It was of crucial importance to policy makers that people were supplied with an adequate supply of nutritional food. Failure to achieve this goal would have had an impact on popular morale and ultimately on Britain's ability to fight. A Ministry of Food was set up to ensure that the population was supplied with necessary food. In a sense this provided a voice for consumers in government. As a result, policy conflicts arose between the Ministry of Agriculture, which protected farming interests, and the Ministry of Food, which defended consumers' interests. The Ministry of Agriculture wanted to increase prices and livestock production. The Ministry of Food sought to control price increases to farmers and to ensure that production was concentrated on foods, such as potatoes and cereals, for direct human consumption.

Moreover, the issue of nutrition was also important. During the war, government scientifically determined the best diet possible from available resources and then used rationing to ensure that everyone had a nutritionally-balanced diet. At the Hot Springs Conference in 1944, government accepted responsibility for attempting to improve the diet and food resources of the population and agreed to set up a national nutritional organisation.

During the war, food was political and food policy was made in a relatively open food policy network. It included a range of departments, such as the Ministries of Food and Agriculture, it recognised the interests and needs of consumers, and it was concerned to develop a food policy that was more comprehensive than an agricultural policy based simply on the interests of farmers.

However, in the period after the war, the food policy community changed. Issues of nutrition and consumer interest became secondary to agricultural interests. The policy network became increasingly closed. Food became depoliticised as government adopted a liberal hands-off approach. Rather than adopting a positive nutritional policy, the government's policy was negative.[2] As long as food was safe – in the limited sense of the word – government would leave individuals' choice of food to the market. People could sell and buy the food that they wanted provided that it was not directly harmful. There are several reasons why this change occurred, resulting in creation of a closed policy community:

● **The impact of post-war food shortages** Immediately after the war ended, Britain was faced with the danger of severe food shortages because worldwide famine was pushing up the price of food. In addition, after the war Britain was chronically short of dollars with which to buy food imports. The crisis meant that the government's primary aim was to increase food production as rapidly as possible. This had three effects. Nutritional policy took very much a second place. The leverage of farmers and of their chief representative body, the NFU, was greatly increased. It was agreed by all major actors within the food policy network, that the immediate goal of food policy had to be increased production. Consequently, the interests of consumers in nutritional policy were squeezed out of the policy process.

● **The increased dominance of farmers and the Ministry of Agriculture** As a result of the changing balance of economic and political power, it was farmers and the Ministry of Agriculture which came to dominate food policy rather than the Ministry of Food. The food policy network was gradually subsumed into the agricultural policy network. The NFU was guaranteed a role whilst no provision was made for inclusion of consumer interests. The dominance of agricultural interests was epitomised by the amalgamation of the Ministry of Food into the Ministry of Agriculture in 1951. Officials at the Ministry of Food warned that 'such a Ministry would be subjected to heavy pressure from the National Farmers' Union at Ministerial level [and] would rapidly degenerate into the kind of department that the Ministry of Agriculture is today, i.e. primarily concerned with look after the Farmers' interests'.[3] To a great extent this is what happened.

● **Growth of the food manufacturing industry** Food manufacturing – the process of turning raw food into processed foods, such as crisps, chips, fishfingers and pies – has become one of the largest and most profitable industries in Britain. The interests of food manufacturers are in purchasing cheap food to which they can add a range of additives in order to sell food at a much higher price. The food industry is not particularly concerned with nutritional or labelling issues. It is more interested in selling food to the consumer. In addition, the size of the food industry, and its levels of profit, mean that the industry has a high level of resources available for lobbying. Since 1945, there have been a number of sector-wide food manufacturer organisations, such as the Food Manufacturer's Federation (FMF) and the Food and Drink Industries Council (FDIC). In 1985, FDIC became the Food and Drink Federation (FDF) and, in 1986, the FMF and the FDF merged. There is also a range of sector-specific bodies. The Butter Information Council and the Sugar Bureau are funded by their respective food industries to carry out research and to provide information. Geoffrey Cannon has highlighted how many MPs have connections with the food industry either through consultancies or directorships. In addition, many members of various government food advisory committees have links with the food industry through either direct employment by or receipt of research grants from the food industry. On top of these political connections, the food industry spends an enormous amount on advertising. According to Cannon, 'In 1985 a quarter of all television advertising was for food, and the total amount of money spent by the food industry in Britain on advertising was just under half a billion pounds.'[4] The food industry is economically powerful and has very close relations with government. Its interests are in ensuring a supply of cheap raw materials and in being able to produce its products with as few limitations as possible. It has little interest in developing a policy concerned with the interests of consumers and nutrition.

Until the 1980s, these factors resulted in the absence of an independent and distinct food policy community. Rather, the food policy community was a combination of three interlinked communities:
● The agricultural policy community, comprising MAFF and the NFU.
● The health and diet community, including the DoH, the Committee on Medical Aspects of Food Policy, the BMA and specialist advisers.
● The food community concerned with issues directly related to the food industry, such as standards of hygiene and labelling, and including MAFF, the food industry through individual companies and groups such as FDIC, advisory committees within MAFF and food scientists and nutritionists.

This network had several significant features. First, it was almost completely dominated by the agricultural community. For reasons outlined above, the food industry did not see its interests as being in conflict with those of agriculture. Before Britain joined the EEC, the domestic system of subsidies ensured that prices of food within Britain were kept relatively low and that the food industry had access to the world market and could therefore import cheap raw materials. Consequently, the food industry rarely felt the need for overt lobbying on food policy. It had access to MAFF and, particularly on issues such as food safety and labelling, was fully consulted.

Whilst the food industry was fully informed, consumers and consumer groups were almost completely excluded from the food policy process. For most of the post-war period, consumer groups were not particularly active and the feeling was that MAFF's cheap food policy served the interests of the consumer and, therefore, consumers themselves did not have to be consulted.

Thus in the period from the 1950s to the 1980s, food policy was made in a relatively closed policy network. Both the food industry and farmers had good contacts with government whilst consumers were largely excluded. There was relatively little disagreement between a range of groups over government food policy. Consequently, food policy was depoliticised. It was believed to be concerned with a range of largely technical advice on nutrition and labelling. The role of government was limited to ensuring that the consumer was safe and people knew how to handle food properly. However, in the 1980s, the food issue began to change, having a direct impact on the food policy community. One issue which particularly highlighted this change was the salmonella in eggs affair.

SALMONELLA AND THE NEW FOOD POLITICS

In the early 1980s, a range of food issues came on to the political agenda and transformed food policy from a technical issue to a highly political one. These issues included heart disease, additives in food, listeria, food irradiation and BSE. One that seemed particularly to inspire the media was salmonella in eggs.

In 1988, this issue became highly political. MAFF had, in fact, known since 1981 that the incidence of salmonella was increasing. Yet the issue did not immediately receive much public attention. The view of the policy community was that salmonella in chickens was inevitable and that as long as consumers were informed about how to cook chickens properly there was no need to take further action. In 1987, both MAFF and the DHSS became aware that there was a link between salmonella and eggs. Their initial reaction was to do nothing. However, as evidence of a link between eggs and salmonella grew stronger, the DoH (as the ministry had by then become) decided in July 1988 to warn hospitals not to give patients raw or undercooked eggs. It was only in November 1988 that the DoH and MAFF agreed to issue a press release warning the general public about the dangers of undercooked eggs.

The strategy of the policy community was to try to keep information and control over the issue within its own network. The community wanted to limit the extent to which information was released in order to avoid political controversy. It discussed what information should be released with insider producer groups, the NFU and the British Eggs Industry Council (BEIC), but did not discuss them with consumer groups. The BEIC in particular did not want information on salmonella and eggs to be released to the general public but was prepared to try to solve the problem through new codes of practice.

The policy community attempted to solve the problem internally but it hit the headlines when a junior minister at the DoH, Edwina Currie, announced that 'most of the egg production of this country, sadly, is now infected with salmonella'. Whether consciously or not, Currie brought to the fore a whole range of pre-existing conflicts within the food policy community. Since May 1988, there had been major conflicts between the DHSS and MAFF. MAFF and its producer group clients argued that, because there was no strong evidence of a link between eggs and salmonella, there was no need to inform the public. The DHSS, on the other hand, thought that MAFF was being too protective towards egg producers and believed that a public health warning should have been issued. Currie's statement made these conflicts public and salmonella emerged as a political issue.

Consequently, the nature of policy making changed from one of agreement to one of conflict. John McGregor, Minister of Agriculture, rebuked Currie, accusing her of damaging the egg industry by giving misleading information. This rebuke was followed by intensive NFU lobbying to have Currie removed and to obtain compensation for the damage she had caused to the egg industry. The NFU's concerted lobbying campaign used all its resources and contacts with MAFF to force government to act. Its six poultry specialists coordinated a nationwide campaign. It wrote to 200 MPs and gave many telephone briefings. The Conservative party's 1922 Executive discussed the issue, decided that Currie would have to resign and passed the information to Currie via the chief whip, David Waddington. In response to this widespread pressure, the government announced a compensation scheme to buy eggs from farmers and Currie resigned.

It appeared that the powerful farmers' lobby had been successful again. However, the reality is much more complex. The salmonella crisis was indicative of a general weakening of farmers, partly as a result of long-term changes in the food policy community. Farmers failed to keep the salmonella issue off the agenda. A policy community which had previously been able to avoid publicity and conflict was now subject to widespread political debate.

Many short-term factors led to the politicisation of salmonella. The extent of the food poisoning outbreaks created a problem with which the community had difficulty coping. The DoH and MAFF had different views on how to deal with the problem. MAFF saw it as a problem for the industry whereas the DoH saw it as a health problem. Consequently, the community no longer had a shared world view and the issue became political as a result of interdepartmental conflict. Various actors resorted to overt political activity when the crisis blew up in the media. It appeared that farmers won by securing compensation and the resignation of Currie. However, the politicisation of this issue was demonstrative of wider changes within the policy community. What was important about this incident was not the specific outcome but the underlying causes of the affair and their long-term impact on the politics of food.

CAUSES OF THE POLITICISATION OF FOOD

The salmonella affair was indicative of a wider politicisation of food which resulted from a number of long-term political and social changes. One was change in the economic position and interests of the food industry. In the 30 years after World War Two, the interests of food manufacturers and farmers largely coincided. Both were well served by government's *laissez-faire* food policy. Food manufacturers had access to cheap food and they made large profits by adding value through the processing procedure.

The economic dominance of food manufacturers was also sustained by Retail Price Maintenance (RPM). RPM was a system whereby manufacturers could determine the prices of goods that were sold in the shops. This kept the retail sector weak and divided, and allowed manufacturers to dominate. Consequently, the British food industry was very successful. Since RPM was abolished by the 1963-64 Home government, the industry's position has been greatly threatened. Small retailers have declined and supermarkets have grown and become more concentrated. Between 1976 and 1987, supermarkets increased their share of the market from 57 to 78 per cent. Consequently, they have been able to challenge the economic dominance of food manufacturers and their political interests.[6] Retailers have been able to force food manufacturers to cut prices. More importantly, because of the competitiveness of the retail sector, supermarkets have been very concerned with consumer interests. Individual retailers, and their trade association, the Retail Consortium, have lobbied government on various food issues including irradiation, BSE and use of BST, the milk hormone. In so doing, they have challenged food producers with consumers' interests.

Where government and food manufacturers have been slow to change, food retailers have been prepared to impose their own regulations. Retailers have moved ahead of government food hygiene regulation and have imposed rigorous standards on the companies that produce food for them. Marks & Spencer has introduced its own system of screening employees suspected of bacterial infection and supermarkets have produced their own labelling schemes which are far ahead of government regulations.

Thus the interests of food manufacturers and food retailers have diverged. No longer is it the case that food manufacturers can achieve the sort of food policy they want without taking any action. Food manufacturers have therefore taken on a much more pro-active role and have thus politicised food policy inadvertently.

In the past 20 years not only have conflicts developed between manufacturers and retailers but also membership of the EC has produced conflict between farmers and manufacturers. It means that farmers' prices are protected through the CAP which artificially raises food prices through import controls. As a result, food manufacturers have lost access to cheap food. Farmers have an interest in maintaining the CAP whilst food manufacturers have an interest in its reform.

Recent decades have also witnessed a decline in the power of farmers, who are much less important economically than they once were. Their decline in numbers suggests that any electoral influence they might have had has also disappeared. Conservative MPs are less attached to rural issues and interests than in the past and there has been some cooling of the relationship between farmers and MAFF. In addition, there have been increasing challenges to British and European agricultural policy on grounds of cost and environmental impact. A growing number of pressure groups, such as FoE, the RSPB, the Campaign for the Protection of Rural Britain and the National Consumers Council, are critical of farmers and farm policy.

The policy community has also been threatened by a range of new groups that have become involved in the politics of food. This has happened in two main ways. Traditional and well-established insider interest groups have started to campaign on food issues. The BMA, which was always part of the policy community, has increasingly lobbied government to take a more active role in preventing food-related disease. Consumer groups and the Child Poverty Action Group have raised the issue of the cost and quality of food. More radical groups, such as the London Food Commission, have also been important in challenging the traditional policy community and questioning the traditional parameters of food policy.

As theorists suggest, increased affluence and the development of NSMs have raised 'post-material' values in relation to food. No longer are people concerned with food supply. Instead, they are more concerned with issues of quality and health, notably in relation to heart disease, salmonella, listeria and BSE. People are also concerned about pesticides and additives in food and there is increased demand for organic products. No longer are consumers satisfied with increased food production as the only objective of government food policy.

Furthermore new technology and scientific discoveries have raised other issues. Scientific development has led both to new problems and to the rediscovery of old ones. The development of factory farming has meant that a large number of animals are kept in confined areas. As a result, disease spreads quickly through stock. Consequently, a high death rate is expected and large doses of antibiotics have to be used in the production of pigs and chickens. Intensive techniques have also resulted in the spread of disease through the food chain. As cattle have been fed parts of sheep, herds have developed BSE. Likewise, chickens have been fed chicken remains thereby reproducing salmonella in the chicken population. New technology has introduced food preservation techniques, such as irradiation. This technique has provoked high levels of opposition from retailers, consumer groups and trade unions and has helped to politicise the issue of food. Increased use of additives, pesticides, and hormones in food production has prompted NSMs and established groups to provide more information on the impact that these chemicals have on humans.

The food policy community that existed in a relatively stable and isolated state for 30 years became threatened in the 1980s by internal and external factors. When faced with problems generated by changing values and new technology, actors within the community took different positions. The DoH and doctors promoted health arguments. MAFF attempted to protect producer interests. Some have argued that this breakdown in consensus produced a new food policy network.

A NEW FOOD POLICY NETWORK?

The factors outlined in this chapter have combined to change the issues and groups involved in food policy. What was once a closed and united policy community dealing with what were seen as technical issues has changed into a wider policy network. The salmonella in eggs incident was not an isolated affair but an indication of ways in which the policy community was changing. Once the issue became critical it demonstrated how food policy had changed. To some extent it accelerated the politicisation of food issues and thus drew more groups into the policy process. This change occurred as a result of a range of social, economic and political factors.

Social change has meant that people are more interested in issues of health and food quality. Post-material values appear to have prompted some food policy changes. Economic change has altered the relative importance of actors within the network. Food manufacturers and farmers are less important economically whilst food retailers have become more important. The latter are prepared to challenge government food policy and to impose their own very stringent standards on both farmers and manufacturers. Politically, the food policy community has been threatened by increasing criticism of the high cost of Britain's agricultural policy and by the New Right's emphasis on consumer rights. Consumers and consumer groups have become increasingly vociferous in their demands and this too has had an impact on food production. In addition, much food policy regulation now comes from Europe. This has further opened up the policy network as the EU has introduced increasingly stringent food regulations and allowed new groups into the policy process.

These changes have meant that new groups have became active in food policy and the relative strength of groups within the network has changed. More importantly, crises in food production have meant that there is no longer a single decision-making centre. In recent years, MAFF and the DoH have taken opposing views and have tried to define new responsibilities. In supporting their own positions, they have opened the community further by bringing in new groups and politicising to a greater degree the issue of food. As a result, government has introduced new food legislation to ensure that food technology and distribution are safe, to prevent misleading labelling, to strengthen existing hygiene laws, to extend controls to new technologies and to introduce powers to make emergency control orders.

Does this mean that the food policy network has changed and that it has been replaced by a new network? It is clear that groups that in the past were passive or not interested in food policy have now become actively involved. There has been pressure from many groups, including consumers, the Institute of Environment Officers, the Food Commission, the BMA and nutritionists. There has also been increased media attention on food issues. Not only has the media been central in highlighting food crises but also it now pays great attention to food, with specialist food programmes and magazines and regular attention to the issue of food in nearly all newspapers. No longer is attention focused merely on recipes but on issues of food quality. There have also been demands for changes in the way food policy is made. The Labour Party has suggested placing responsibility for food policy in a ministry for consumer affairs. To some extent change has already happened. The DoH is no longer prepared to accept MAFF's lead in the policy process. It has also been much more active in giving a role to doctors and nutritionists in policy making. MAFF itself has made some changes and has created a new advisory committee concerned with food-borne illnesses. MAFF has also created a consumer panel to convey views on food protection to the ministry.

However, it is important not to exaggerate the degree of change. Despite pressure group concerns, the government has lifted the ban on irradiated food. The House of Commons Social Services Select Committee found that government knew of the problem of listeria in 1987 but did not issue a warning to pregnant women until February 1989. The government has also been accused of being slow to act over the issue of BSE. Some maintain that its response is still not sufficiently radical to ensure that consumers are properly informed. The disease was discovered in 1986 but only made notifiable in 1988. Despite worries about calves being infected with the disease, government only banned the use of calves' offal in July 1994. In the case of the hormone BST, the government has refused to reveal which farms are using it thereby denying consumers the right to choose whether or not to buy milk that contains BST. The government has also refused to ban use of the hormone.

There is still a high degree of exclusion of consumers. The NCC has revealed that consumer groups find it difficult to get on to consultation lists, and that they are only consulted after decisions have been made and are therefore not given sufficient time to respond to government policy. MAFF has continued to be secretive over food issues. Its consumer board contains four representatives nominated by government-funded consumer bodies and only one nominated by an independent group. Radical groups, such as Parents for Safe Food and the Food Commission, continue to be excluded.

Nevertheless, the food policy community is not what it was. The whole issue is much more political, more groups have become involved and the old consensus has disappeared. Despite continued exclusion, the policy network is more open than in the past.

CONCLUSION

What is interesting about food policy is that it shows that relationships between groups and government can change quite dramatically. However, the cause of change in policy and policy networks is frequently not pressure group activity but wider social and political change. Changes in society, politics and economics have affected the position and resources of groups and changed the way that policy makers and the wider public perceive problems. To an extent, major changes have occurred not because of anything that pressure groups have consciously chosen to do. Instead, new issues, new economic relations and changes in values and interests have changed relationships within the policy network and created new problems which have divided it. In this way, new groups have entered the policy network and changed policy.

NOTES

1 M Mills, 'Networks and Policy on Diet and Disease', in D Marsh and R A W Rhodes (eds) Policy Networks in British Government (Oxford University Press, Oxford, 1992).
2 M Mills, The Politics of Dietary Health (Dartmouth, Aldershot, 1993).
3 Quoted in M Smith 'From Policy Community to Issue Network: Salmonella in Eggs and the New Politics of Food', Public Administration, 69, 1991, p.238.
4 G Cannon, The Politics of Food (Century, London, 1987), p.73.
5 D Hughes, A Roy and M Chittenden, 'Currie, Eggs and Chicken', Sunday Times, 18 December 1988.
6 C Gardener and J Sheppard, Consuming Passion; the Rise of Retail Culture (Unwin Hyman, London, 1989).

8 THE CHANGING HEALTH POLICY NETWORK

In the post-war period, health policy is an area in which a relatively closed and integrated policy network has developed between doctors and government, in particular the health department. This policy network placed doctors in a very strong position. Their close relationship with the department gave them a high degree of influence over policy. Their position was underpinned by a broad consensus that doctors had clinical autonomy. This effectively meant that they could manage the NHS and determine how resources were used on the ground. During the 1980s and 1990s, this policy community has been placed under great strain. It has been affected by social change, economic decline and ideological shifts. Social change has meant that more groups have attempted to become involved in health policy. Economic decline has increased pressure on health budgets. These factors have encouraged a New Right-influenced government to challenge doctors' autonomy. This chapter examines threats to the health policy community and the extent to which it has changed in recent years.

SOCIAL CHANGE AND THE POLICY COMMUNITY

The health policy community developed after the war placed doctors in an extremely influential position. However, despite the degree of consensus over health policy aims and the particular roles of doctors and government there were a number of conflicts. These conflicts became particularly great during the 1970s when some of the fundamental problems of the welfare state became increasingly apparent.

To begin with there was increased conflict between health professionals' desire to maintain autonomy and government's ever more determined desire to control costs. Professional autonomy meant that doctors should be free to decide who needs what treatment, when and how. However, that degree of autonomy requires almost unlimited funds. Government, on the other hand, was being forced by economic crisis to cut public expenditure which created the need for rationing of certain treatments. The problem with the health compromise made at the start of the post-war period was that it divorced 'political decisions about the NHS budget from professional decisions about the allocation of resources to individual patients'.[1] With rising costs and increasing economic problems, government found it difficult to maintain control of health-care spending.

As a result of rationing, NHS efficiency and effectiveness were called into question. Costs rose but many people with chronic and minor illnesses found that they had to wait much longer for treatment. Quality of care was also increasingly questioned. This threatened to the policy community in two ways. First, consumers began to take an increasing interest in health care and demands were made through community health councils and pressure groups, such as MIND, that the patients' interests be taken more into account.[2] Second, attempts were made to introduce much greater managerial control. For the first time managerial criteria were introduced in the distribution of NHS resources and this threatened the position of doctors.

Increasingly, then, the health policy community was threatened by consumers and managers. There was also growing conflict between health professionals inside the network and those who were excluded. The health policy community was very much two-tiered. The primary community comprised almost exclusively doctors and health department officials. The secondary community was made up of individuals affected by particular issues. It included nurses, health professionals, such as physiotherapists and radiologists, and, to some extent, trade unions representing ancillary workers. Patients tended to be excluded from the network. Increasingly those who were involved in the secondary community, and largely only consulted on issues of pay, demanded to be involved more generally in health policy making. They wanted a greater input into management and the policy process. In particular, health service unions grew in both size and activity. They became increasingly militant over issues of pay and this militancy spread into central areas of health policy.

Despite conflicts and demands from potential entrants, the health policy community remained largely intact during the 1970s. The consensus on the role of doctors and health policy was questioned but not undermined. The real threat to the policy community came in 1979 with the election of a Conservative government influenced by New Right ideology.

THE THATCHER GOVERNMENTS AND THE
HEALTH POLICY COMMUNITY

For the Thatcher governments, one of the key problems of the NHS was not underfunding but inefficient use of resources. To a large extent, although they did not say it, this was the product of the health policy community. Government blamed special interests, particularly doctors, for continually demanding an increase in resources and then not subjecting their use to sufficient managerial control. Government policy in the early 1980s therefore aimed to increase managerial control. It sought to control costs by increasing efficiency and, if necessary, by breaking the policy community.[3]

However, government policy was initially concerned to maintain the existing structure of the NHS, and to protect NHS expenditure. However, policy makers were faced with demographic trends which increased demands on the health service and with new medical technology which raised costs faster than the rate of inflation. Therefore the only way that government could maintain levels of service without substantially increasing costs was through increasing efficiency.

In order to develop a system for managing the NHS, the first Thatcher government in 1983 invited four businessmen, under the chairmanship of Sir Roy Griffiths, to inquire into the 'effective use and management of manpower and related resources in the National Health Service'. Their report recommended creation of a management board and introduction of general managers at each NHS level. In addition, the role of clinical doctors in local management was to be increased.[4]

These reforms had a significant impact on the power of doctors and the health policy community. Even the way in which the report was compiled challenged the health policy community. Rather than reforms being developed by the community, a group of outsiders was appointed to examine NHS reform. This was an important change in the normal process of health policy making. The changes recommended by Griffiths' team also challenged doctors' clinical autonomy. Managers were given a greater say in resource distribution and this reduced the ability of doctors to decide which areas should be given priority. As a result, managers can now challenge doctors. The system of consensus management which had characterised the first 40 years of the NHS was undermined, indicating an important shift in power within health policy.[5]

Griffiths did not solve the problems of the NHS. Demands for increased spending continued as did criticisms of the service and of government's handling of reform. After the 1987 general election the NHS appeared to reach crisis point. Increased wage costs generated a severe spending crisis at the end of the year. Conflict between ministers and consultants reached a very high level. The president of the Royal College of Surgeons accused the Thatcher government of providing insufficient resources to carry out operations. For its part, the government accused consultants of not implementing the new management system. However, the combination of media and medical pressure forced the government to back down and to provide the NHS with an extra £1.1 billion.

These events indicated to Prime Minister Thatcher and Secretary of State John Moore that the Griffiths' report had not solved underlying problems in the NHS and that the cash injection was only a short-term solution. As a result, in January 1988 Thatcher announced a thorough review of the NHS with the aim of increasing value for money. It was intended that the review should consider all options. Ideas, such as hotel charges and tax relief on private insurance, which had previously been ruled out, were back on the agenda.

This review also had important implications for the health policy community. It did not involve the usual policy community actors but was made up of civil servants and ministers chosen by the Prime Minister and advisers drawn largely from New Right think tanks. Most importantly, the review was directed by the Prime Minister who was prepared to use her authority to ignore the traditional community and to challenge the policy consensus. The review was conducted entirely without consultation with key medical pressure groups. No representatives of either the BMA or the Royal Colleges were included and even the role of the DoH was peripheral. The Prime Minister believed that if doctors were involved, they would merely hinder the review by raising objections and pointing out the problems of radical reform.

Despite the Prime Minister's capture of the review process, the White Paper, *Working for Patients*, published in January 1989, was less radical than many had either hoped or feared. The proposed reforms did not fundamentally undermine the NHS 'as we know it'. The Prime Minister was constrained by popular support for the NHS and a lack of constituencies within it which could be used to implement change.

The central intention of the reform was to introduce some form of market into the NHS by separating funding and provision of health care. District Health Authorities (DHAs) were to be given the power to offer contracts to, and to buy blocks of services from, competing hospitals. In addition, the government proposed that hospitals could become self-governing trusts which could set their own conditions of service and be permitted to sell services to other health authorities. As a result, there would be competition between hospitals. Furthermore, certain larger GP practices would be given budgets with which they could also purchase services. The intention was to create a system of internal markets whilst continuing to provide free health care at the point of delivery.[6]

A NEW HEALTH POLICY COMMUNITY

It is clear that in reforming health policy and in changing the NHS management structure, the third Thatcher government was prepared to challenge the existing policy community. Through implementation of a system of general management and increased use of performance indicators, it challenged the notion of clinical autonomy. As the House of Commons Social Services Select Committee pointed out:

> In the context of the NHS philosophy of offering diagnoses and treatment without reference to the patient's ability to pay and an inexorable rise in the scope and cost of diagnostic tools and treatment available, the time has come to question the doctor's right to commit resources without reference to the NHS's ability to meet the commitment.

As a result of the reforms, managers have greater control of the work of practitioners and there is also greater peer review of practitioners' work. The distribution of merit awards to consultants, for example, 'will be determined not just by doctors but also the managers who hold the contracts', and in opted-out hospitals management determination of pay and conditions is increasing.[7] *Working for Patients* was concerned to make doctors accountable 'for the consequences of their decisions in terms of both costs and quality' and therefore sought to make each practitioner subject to a medical audit of regular and formalised peer review. Central to the reforms was an attempt to change the distribution of power in the NHS by separating managers from clinicians, and by removing the right of doctors to veto certain decisions. According to Wistow, 'the changes of the mid-1980s and the 1989 White Paper do represent a significant expansion of management authority from the top down and contain significant challenges to medical autonomy.'[8]

Government also claimed that the reforms increase the power of consumers. The internal market is making hospitals more competitive, and presumably more responsive, to consumer demands. Through internal markets money follows patients giving DHAs an incentive to attract patients. In addition, obstacles to changing GPs have been reduced and the proportion of GP income deriving from capitation fees has been increased, thereby making it essential for practices to attract patients. However, the danger is that in the reformed NHS some DHAs will not provide certain services, patients will have to travel further for treatment, and costs for some services will rise. Moreover, there is no provision for increased consumer representation in either policy making or administration: 'The White Paper intends a model of consumerism based on choice through the market place rather than participation in decision making'.[9]

Changes in the policy community have also taken place. Policy making has shifted from a consensual to a conflictual mode. To an extent recent governments have been prepared to exclude traditional members of the policy community and include new groups, such as New Right think tanks. None of the Royal Colleges was consulted either before or after publication of the White Paper. As a consequence, relations between doctors and government have deteriorated. As the BMA, and to some extent the Royal Colleges, have been prevented from operating within the policy community, they have had to adopt more overt, pluralistic forms of lobbying. In 1989, the BMA launched a concerted campaign against government reforms using posters, direct lobbying, contact with MPs, threats of mass resignation and use of the media. Their poster campaign even resorted to direct insults of the Secretary of State for Health, Kenneth Clarke. In July 1989, the BMA voted not to cooperate with implementation of government reform proposals on internal markets, hospital contracts, self-governing trusts and GP practice budgets. The result was that in April 1990 a new GP contract was imposed on the medical profession.[10]

Doctors have now accepted the reforms but, at the same time, continue to criticise government handling of the NHS. Similarly, consultants continue to oppose the establishment of NHS trusts. In order to ensure implementation of its reforms, policy makers did, in the end, consult GPs and made a number of small concessions on payments for vaccinations, screening and minor operations.

Undoubtedly, then, the third Thatcher government did change the nature of the health policy community. Wistow concludes that, 'Taken together, the package of proposals ... appears to represent a ministerial commitment to achieve a substantial transfer of power and influence from medicine to management.'[11] In addition, there has been a fragmentation of power with decision making being moved from the centre to district and, in the case of trusts, hospital level. Recent governments have attacked the consensus and ideology of the policy community by questioning clinical autonomy and removing doctors' veto over both decisions of implementation and of wider policy. Consequently, conflict and new groups have entered the network and undermined the closed policy community that previously existed. Yet, at the same time, this has not become a loose issue network. Doctors are still important to the process of making and implementing policy, and structures of institutionalised access still exist. In fact, Secretary of State for Health, Virginia Bottomley, admitted in June 1992 that if government had consulted more widely during the policy review it might not have faced such substantial problems in convincing doctors that the new policy has benefits. As Day and Klein suggest, 'Following the confrontational crisis, it was in the self-interest of Government to be conciliatory and to revert to administering policy through the medical profession.'[12]

The Thatcher years are interesting in analysing the role of pressure groups. At least in the 1980s, health policy was an area in which the demands of established pressure groups were ignored because of the clear political goals of government. Thatcher was prepared to use her political authority and capital to challenge an established policy community by making policy outside of it. She realised that if reform was left to the community it would be emasculated and thus she demonstrated that political actors could take decisions without the support of the key interest groups. Nevertheless, this did have costs. Thatcher, if not constrained by the policy community, was constrained by public opinion, and thus the radicalism of policy change was limited. In by-passing the community she created a high level of ill-feeling amongst doctors and made the development of policy and, in particular, its implementation, more difficult. Doctors could not be completely ignored, and although management's role has been increased, doctors still have a major impact on policy and implementation.

THE MAJOR GOVERNMENTS AND HEALTH POLICY

The Major governments have continued the policy introduced by
Thatcher. Increasing numbers of hospitals are becoming NHS trusts
and more GPs are choosing to manage their own budgets. By April
1994, the number of NHS trusts was 389. However, political battles
within the health service are continuing and the consensus that
existed in the post-war period has yet to be re-established.

There are two views on the impact of reform on the NHS. One is that
increased emphasis on managers rather than practitioners is raising
bureaucratic costs. Some estimates suggest that expenditure on
administration has increased by £3 billion and has therefore doubled
since 1987-88. As a result, administration is now consuming 11 per
cent of the NHS budget, the highest proportion ever. Even a Conservative cabinet minister, John Redwood, has claimed that government
reforms have resulted in an increase in senior managers from 1200 in
1988 to 13,300 in 1991 whilst the number of nurses has dropped by
9000. A number of these managers have been appointed to operate
the new internal market. Others result from the re-classification as
managers of some of the higher nursing grades. The reforms are also
criticised for creating a two-tier health service. Those who are patients
at practices where doctors are fundholders are more likely to receive
treatment quickly than those registered at non-fundholding practices.
Hospital trusts now sell services and so will provide them to GPs who
have the funds to pay. Others have to wait on long waiting lists.

An alternative view is that the reforms have had little impact.
However, it is argued that now that market mechanisms are in
place[13] the potential for gain has been established. With more information and better use of resources in the new market system than
in the past, decision making in resource allocation will be improved.

Whatever their merits, the health service reforms have created conflicting interests within the health policy network. Whereas in the past
key actors had common goals, these have now disappeared. On one
side, government and NHS managers argue that introduction of a
business ethos has greatly improved NHS efficiency. Competition in
the provision of health care ensures effective resource use and will
therefore cut costs. On the other hand, opposition groups, such as
doctors, consultants and opposition parties, argue that certain groups
of people, such as the elderly, are unable to receive hospital treatment

on cost grounds. Consultants argue that the internal market has resulted in extra bureaucracy not greater efficiency. According to the Chairman of the National Health Service Consultants:

> Unless we are released from the nonsense of business plans, marketing, contracting, chasing extra-contractual referrals and so on, cutting these posts will lead to health professionals having to devote even more time to administration. We might do it more simply and cheaply, without the fog of management jargon and the mounds of paper which now engulf us.[14]

The BMA has been even more militant in its opposition. In 1993, its chairman was deposed apparently for supporting a softly-softly approach to criticism of the NHS reforms. He was replaced by Dr Alexander Macara who favours a high-profile campaign to indicate to the public problems with GP fundholding. He argued that it was necessary to be vigorous in persuading the Health Secretary to re-examine the need for change. In July 1994, he claimed that the reforms had reduced NHS morale by giving commercial and managerial criteria precedence over clinical judgements.

However, the result of the BMA's campaign is that doctors are excluded from DoH talks on restructuring the NHS. The BMA is not officially represented on working committees set up to examine the impact of changing the regional organisation of the NHS.

THE NEW HEALTH POLICY COMMUNITY

Conflicts that have occurred in the 1990s indicate the extent to which the health policy community has changed. When Bevan established the NHS after World War Two, he constructed a careful consensus. Both parties accepted the outlines of the NHS and doctors and consultants, despite initial opposition, recognised the need to provide free health care in return for a considerable degree of clinical and, in effect, managerial autonomy. The reforms introduced since 1989 have destroyed that consensus and have created at least four sets of distinct interests:

● **Government** Recent governments have demanded efficiency, that is, increasing health-care provision whilst restraining cost increases.

● **Managers** Managers are concerned with efficient use of resources at regional and hospital levels and see their role as making providers of health care competitive in the new internal market.

● **Doctors and health-care professionals** Doctors and other NHS professionals are concerned to retain as much control as possible over resource distribution within the NHS.

● **Patients** By establishing certain rights for the consumers of health care – patients – Conservative governments have effectively introduced a new interest in health-care policy making. The purpose of the internal market is to provide consumer power by giving patients a choice of health-care providers. In principle, patients can go where the best service is provided. In addition, the first Major government created the Patient's Charter, which tabled a clear and distinct set of rights for patients concerning health-care quality and waiting times.

Thus, what was once a consensual and closed policy community with relatively few interests has become much more open and conflictual. With so many competing interests in the health policy domain, it is more difficult for it to remain technical rather than political. The likelihood is that the network will now remain more open and that health policy will be more controversial as health professionals, managers and patients articulate a range of conflicting interests to the DoH.

Disintegration of the health policy community has been the result of many factors:

● **Economic decline** Britain's relative economic decline has increased the necessity to control public expenditure. As one of the largest areas of government spending, health has been subject to clear restraint.

● **Technological change** New techniques and medicines have meant that the NHS can provide many more treatments than in the past. People can have heart transplants, be cured of a range of cancers, and be treated for diseases that were previously killers. As a result, demand for health care has increased greatly thereby pushing up costs.

● **Demographic change** An ageing population has increased pressure on NHS resources.

● **Social change** As people have become more aware of their rights, they have demanded more as patients and as consumers of health care. This has raised costs, but, perhaps more importantly, it has led to increased questioning of professionals. Social change has also resulted in unionisation of health workers, such as nurses and auxiliaries, and has meant that doctors have lost their monopoly position as the sole important interest group in the NHS.

● **Political change** The impact of Thatcherism on the health policy network has probably been as great as any other contributory factor. The New Right rejected the health-care consensus and sought to replace dominant health-care professionals with managers as a means of promoting effective resource use.

In a sense, the New Right has always been in a Catch-22 situation as regards the NHS. Ideologically, it is opposed to most of the principles underpinning it. However, Conservative governments have always realised that the NHS is extremely popular. Therefore, they have been limited in the types of reforms that could be introduced. As a result, they have attempted to control costs and increase efficiency through market mechanisms whilst at the same time maintaining the basic principle of the NHS: that it is free at the point of delivery.

CONCLUSION

Doctors were in an very powerful position during most of the post-war period. The health-policy consensus meant that if they were pre-pared to provide health care free at the point of delivery, then they could manage the NHS on a day-to-day basis. However, due to eco-nomic, social and political change, pressure to control costs increased. As a result, government attempted to introduce a management ethos into the NHS. The impact of this change is that consensus was under-mined by introduction of a range of conflicting interests. A closed policy community has been replaced by a more open and conflictual network. Simultaneously, doctors' influence in the making of health policy has been reduced. Competing sets of interests now try to influ-ence policy, and government is more prepared than in the past to ignore doctors' demands. Change in the health policy community indicates the way in which group power is never inherent. Even when groups are well resourced, their ability to use those resources often depends on the perceptions of the government of the day.

NOTES

1 R Klein, 'The Politics of Ideology vs the Reality of Politics: The Case of Britain's National Health Service in the 1980s', *Milbank Quarterly*, 62, p.86.
2 R Klein, *The Politics of the NHS* (Longman, London, 1989).
3 G Wistow, 'The National Health Service', in D Marsh and R A W Rhodes (eds), *Implementing Thatcherite Policies: Audit of an Era* (Open University Press, Milton Keynes, 1994).
4 S Harrison, *Managing the National Health Service* (Chapman Hall, London, 1988).
5 Ibid., p.72.
6 I Holliday, *The NHS Transformed: A Guide to the Health Reforms* (Baseline Books, Manchester, 1992).
7 A Maynard, *Wither the National Health Service?* (Centre for Health Economics, University of York), p.23.
8 G Wistow, 'The Health Service Policy Community: Professionals Pre-Eminent of Under Challenge?', in D Marsh and R A W Rhodes (eds), *Policy Networks in British Government* (Oxford University Press, Oxford, 1992).
9 Ibid. p.68.
10 P Day and R Klein, 'Constitutional and Distributional Conflict in British Medical Practice, 1911-1991', *Political Studies*, 50, 1992, p.469.
11 Wistow, 'Health Service Policy Community', op cit. p.71.
12 Day and Klein, op cit. p.475.
13 N Barr, H Glennerster and J Le Grand, *Reform and the National Health* (LSE discussion paper, London).
14 *Times*, 26 September 1993.

9 PRESSURE GROUPS AND THE BRITISH POLITICAL SYSTEM

In pluralist theory, pressure groups are essential to the political system. They prevent the state from having a monopoly of power and ensure that people are able to influence government between elections. In other words pressure groups are a bulwark against 'elective dictatorship'. The problem with this view is that it assumes that most pressure groups have access to the political system and that resources are relatively well dispersed throughout it. The notion of policy networks is useful because it questions this view. The policy networks approach highlights the deficiency of the traditional approach to pressure groups. It is for this reason that this approach has been used in this book.

POLICY NETWORKS AND THE POLITICAL SYSTEM

When examining pressure groups, it is vital to look not only at what they do and what resources they have, but also at the context in which they operate and how they are perceived. That context includes:
● the present political situation – what issues are important.
● the historical context – what groups and issues have been important in the past and the ways in which they have affected the policy-making process.
● the ideological context – the political priorities of government.
● the economic and social context – the impact of economic and social factors on the resources and perceptions of groups.
Hence groups are not inherently powerful. Their influence changes according to the existing situation and the way in which they are perceived by government.

It is also important not to privilege pressure groups in understanding policy outcomes. Pressure groups are only one factor in explaining policy. Sufficient consideration must be given to the role of government, and Whitehall more generally. Government actors, both politicians and civil servants, frequently have their own interests and their own policy goals. They are also very well resourced. They have a high level of legitimacy, they have the bureaucratic resources to develop and implement policies and, if necessary, they have control over coercive powers to ensure that policy is carried out. Government can survive without pressure groups but pressure groups cannot survive without government. There are many occasions when governments have ignored pressure groups and the adverse effect has been minimal. An example is the Conservatives and trade unions since 1979.

Nevertheless, government cannot afford to ignore all pressure groups all the time. A government's legitimacy can be impaired if it is continually opposed by a broad range of pressure groups. Therefore governments try to ensure that they are supported by some groups. Moreover, the process of policy making is much simpler if pressure groups are involved in the development and implementation of policy. Without pressure groups, government has to gather all information itself and develop the machinery for policy implementation. Pressure groups can provide an alternative to formal administrative machinery for developing and implementing policy. A wide range of policies, for example in the spheres of health or education, cannot be delivered without the cooperation of those responsible for delivery. Consequently, government has made many concessions to both doctors and teachers in the process of reforming health and education policy.[1]

Yet pressure groups are still highly dependent on government. If they are to influence policy, it is best that they are insiders. They must, therefore, abide by rules of the game. In this way, they obtain information from government on policy developments and are usually guaranteed consultation. However, being an insider does not ensure influence and frequently insider groups are prepared to accept defeat on many occasions in order to be successful on relatively few.

It is, therefore, extremely difficult to make generalisations about the power of pressure groups. The impact that they have depends on context, policy area, time and, perhaps most importantly, type of relationship that they have with government. This book has highlighted the different types of network which exist in different policy areas. Relationships between groups and government can vary from very closed policy communities to very open issue networks. The nature of these networks affects the influence that pressure groups have. It also affects policy outcomes.

In a closed policy community there is consensus over desirable policy outcomes and pressure groups are likely to be involved in detailed policy making. Groups which disagree with the consensus are excluded from the policy process. Thus, in a policy community policy outcomes are relatively predictable, the number of groups involved is very limited and change is difficult to achieve. As a result, a small number of groups may be very powerful whilst others could be almost completely powerless.

In an issue network, many groups are likely to be involved in the policy process and there will be little consensus both within and outside government on desired policy goals. Consequently, policy outcomes are unpredictable and likely to change frequently as different groups move in and out of the policy arena. The identity of influential groups is likely to fluctuate and it is unlikely that any single group will be able to exercise a dominant influence over the policy process.

POLICY NETWORKS AND CHANGE

One factor that this book emphasises is the way in which policy networks – particularly some closed policy communities – have changed in recent years. Although policy communities are difficult to change, they are not immune to outside forces and British politics has been affected by some significant changes in the past 20 years.

Of crucial importance has been the collapse of the social democratic consensus and the rise of New Right ideology. This ideological change has challenged many of the ideas of established policy communities. Thatcher was prepared to use her authority as prime minister directly to undermine a range of policy communities particularly, but not solely, in the area of welfare policy. Alongside changes in the health policy community outlined in this book have been changes in education, local government and the industrial relations network.

Indeed, New Right ideology and the Thatcher governments were crucial in changing a range of policy areas. The New Right believes that groups distort the democratic process and result in an inefficient distribution of resources. The Thatcher governments' view was that decisions should be made in parliament by elected representatives and not by special interests in policy networks. Consequently, many traditional interests were challenged. However, rather than pluralism replacing policy networks, new interests, such as think tanks, were given a privileged place in the policy process.

Networks have also been affected by social and economic change. The major social and economic transformations that have occurred in Britain in the past 20 years have affected the respective resources of a range of pressure groups and this has led to the rise of NSMs. These are interesting because they have the potential to change the whole nature of pressure group politics. NSMs tend to represent new interests, organise in unusual manners and operate outside the traditional rules of the game and policy networks. Again, however, it is difficult to generalise. NSMs represent a range of different groups, some of which have become relatively integrated into the policy process whilst others have remained very much outsiders. Consequently, it is difficult to assess the impact of NSMs. However, what appears to be important is that although they may have had limited effects on particular policies or made little inroads into established policy networks, they have changed the political agenda.

NSMs have been effective in two ways. They have raised new problems and have therefore had some success in shifting the political agenda in certain policy areas, even if they have not changed policy networks. Issues raised by NSMs, such as the quality of food and the environmental impact of farming, have had to be addressed by the food and agricultural network. Likewise all the established political parties have had to respond to the environmental movement.

In addition, although NSMs have had a limited impact in the political arena, they have been far more effective in the social. NSMs may not, so far, have been very successful in challenging the way politicians behave but they have had some success in changing popular attitudes to women, gays and the environment. Thus, the impact of NSMs has been greatest on individual lifestyles rather than on the traditional conceptions of politics. This is important because it is a way of bypassing the traditional power structures within which pressure groups normally act and means that groups can have influence without having access to policy networks.

A further factor that has caused network change is the increasing importance of Europe. Now much policy that was once the responsibility of national government has shifted to the European level. This has changed the nature of policy networks as they have had to become transnational. Moreover, the relative openness of EU policy making has made it more difficult to maintain closed policy networks.

Again, this has affected the way pressure groups behave. It means that they no longer have to rely on traditional national closed networks but have a range of access points in the EU which may be more receptive to their demands. In particular, we can see how issues relating to the equality of women and environmental issues have been successfully pursued through the ECJ. The Maastricht Treaty has also made the EP more powerful which has demonstrated that it is receptive to traditionally-excluded groups.

Nearly all policy networks have been affected by these pressures for change. Nevertheless what is apparent is that some networks have changed more than others. Whilst there have been major changes in the health and food networks, networks in areas such as agriculture, energy and even transport have been much more stable. Two factors explain this divergence. One is the nature of the individual network and the second is the degree of political will applied to reform. Whether a network changes depends on its ability to remain relatively depoliticised. In a period of economic decline when the role of the state in welfare became central to political debate, it was very difficult for the health policy network to remain apolitical. The consensus which underpinned it broke down. Likewise in the food policy network, food scares and changing attitudes towards food led to the politicisation of policy.

However, whilst politicisation of food changed the nature of the food policy network, it has not really opened up the agricultural policy network. An explanation of this difference may be found in the actors involved in each network. The food network contained a range of interests – agricultural, industrial, health, and consumer. When faced with new situations and new demands each of these interests had conflicting commitments and this led to conflict in the network. As a result, it was relatively easy to change. The agricultural network contained mainly farming and agricultural interests and, despite external pressure, largely managed to maintain a consensus and to prevent new groups from entering. Consequently, despite some changes in policy, farmers still receive a high degree of subsidy and the policy community is more or less intact.

Political will is also an important factor. To a large extent, prime ministers have lacked the will or interest to tackle the agricultural policy community. In the case of networks in health and education, Thatcher was determined to challenge the status quo. She consciously undermined previously dominant actors – doctors and teachers – and introduced new actors, such as managers, school governors and, to a limited extent, patients and parents into the networks. The fact that the prime minister wanted change made it very difficult for these policy networks to resist.

THE CHANGING ROLE OF PRESSURE GROUPS

Pressure groups are undoubtedly extremely important in understanding the political process. However, traditional approaches have often oversimplified the role of groups and exaggerated their degree of influence on policy. The extent of pressure group influence depends on the nature of its relationship with government and the interests and resources of government actors. Policy networks differ by policy area. The nature of a network affects how policy is made and therefore affects the influence of pressure groups.

It is also important to realise that many of the networks that have existed in Britain developed within the context of the peculiar social, economic and political conditions which existed in the years following World War Two. Those conditions have changed with Britain's economic decline, the rise of the New Right and major social and economic change. This has affected the resources of groups and the way in which they are perceived. It is for this reason that many of the post-war networks are starting to change. New groups are becoming important, and established groups are having to adopt new tactics. In these circumstances, a new set of policy networks is developing.

A FUTURE FOR PRESSURE GROUPS?

It has been argued that increasing disillusionment with traditional politics is pushing more and more people into pressure-group politics. In these circumstances, the future for pressure groups is unclear. Some believe that we are now entering a new era of pressure-group politics. To some extent, the 1980s and 1990s have been a period of increased pluralism. More groups are involved in politics and more people are involved in pressure groups. People are leaving political parties and opinion polls show widespread mistrust of government and politicians. Consequently, pressure groups could be increasingly important modes of expressing political grievances.

Nevertheless, it has to be remembered that whilst membership of political parties is in decline, recent years have seen an increased vitality in party politics. Similarly, electoral turnout shows no sign of declining. Parties control government and government continues to have the resources to ignore pressure groups when it chooses.

In many ways, pressure groups have not done particularly well in the past 15 years. The power of professional groups in health and education has been undermined by increased managerialism. The power of trades unions and, to some extent, manufacturing industry has been reduced by economic restructuring and political challenges. During the 1980s and 1990s, Conservative governments have been less prepared to consult interest groups in preparing policy and legislation. One result is an increasing amount of poorly-drafted legislation which subsequently requires substantial amendment. Examples are the Criminal Justice Bill of 1994, the Child Support Act 1993 and the Financial Services Act 1986.[2]

In addition, although many new groups are involved in politics, either they have limited access to government and consequently minimal impact on policy or they are still outsiders. Networks might be changing, but new ones are forming which suggests that traditional forms of government/pressure group relations may continue even if the groups themselves change.

NOTE

1 I Holliday, *The NHS Transformed: A Guide to the Health Reforms* (Baseline Books, Manchester, 1992); C Chitty, *The Education System Transformed: A Guide to the School Reforms* (Baseline Books, Manchester, 1992).
2 G Mather, 'The Market, Accountability and the Civil Service', paper presented to the Public Administration Committee Annual Conference, University of York, 4-6 September 1994.

A BRIEF GUIDE TO FURTHER READING

There are literally hundreds of book on pressure group politics. Perhaps the most useful introductions are W Grant, *Pressure Groups, Politics and Democracy in Britain* (Philip Allen, London, 1989) and JJ Richardson, *Pressure Groups* (Oxford University Press, Oxford, 1993). A more advanced account is provided in A G Jordan and JJ Richardson, *Government and Pressure Groups in Britain* (Clarendon Press, Oxford, 1987).

On theoretical and conceptual issues it is worth looking at D Marsh and R Rhodes, *Policy Networks in British Government* (Oxford University Press, Oxford, 1992) and MJ Smith, *Pressure, Power and Policy* (Harvester Wheatsheaf, Hemel Hempstead, 1993). The most useful book on corporatism is A Cawson, *Corporatism and Political Theory* (Basil Blackwell, Oxford, 1986).

An assessment of the impact of social change in Britain is made in F Green, *The Restructuring of the British Economy* (Harvester Wheatsheaf, Hemel Hempstead, 1989). The impact of Europe on pressure groups is comprehensively examined in S Mazey and JJ Richardson (eds), *Lobbying in the European Community* (Oxford University Press, Oxford, 1993). The best assessment of the impact of the New Right is made in A Gamble, *The Free Economy and the Strong State: The Politics of Thatcherism*, second edition, (Macmillan, London, 1994).

There are countless case studies of pressure group behaviour. Among the most useful are W Grant, *Business and Politics in Britain*, second edition (Macmillan, London, 1994); D Marsh, *The New Politics of Trade Unionism* (Macmillan, London, 1992); M Mills, *The Politics of Dietary Health* (Dartmouth, Aldershot, 1993); P Lowe and J Goyder, *Environmental Groups in Politics* (Allen and Unwin, London, 1983); R Klein, *The Politics of the NHS* (Longman, London, 1989), MJ Smith, *The Politics of Agricultural Support* (Dartmouth, Aldershot, 1990); I Holliday, *The NHS Transformed* (Baseline Books, Manchester, 1992).

The best books on new social movements are Alan Scott, *Ideology and New Social Movements* (Unwin Hyman, London, 1990) and R Dalton and M Kuchler, *Challenging the Political Order* (Polity Press, Cambridge, 1990).

INDEX

IN THE SAME SERIES